Beyond Persuasion

THE HEALTHCARE
MANAGER'S
GUIDE TO
STRATEGIC
COMMUNICATION

Patricia J. Parsons

Beyond Persuasion

The Healthcare Manager's Guide to Strategic Communication

Health Administration Press, Chicago, Illinois

Your board staff or clients may benefit from this book's insight. For more information on quantity discounts, contact the Health Administration Press Marketing Manager at (312) 424–9470.

05 04 03 02 01   5 4 3 2 1

Library of Congress Cataloging-in-Publication Data

Parsons, Patricia J.
Beyond persuasion : the healthcare manager's guide to strategic communication / by Patricia J. Parsons.
    p. cm.
    Includes bibliographical references.
    ISBN 1-56793-152-9
    1. Health services administration. 2. Communication in medicine. 3. Communication in management. I. Title.
RA971 .P2754   2001
362.1'068'4—dc21   2001016869

The paper used in this publication meets the minimum requirements of American National Standard for Information Sciences—Permanence of Paper for Printed Library Materials, ANSI Z39.48–1984.™

Project manager: Cami Cacciatore; Book design: Matt Avery; Cover design: Anne LoCascio

Health Administration Press
A division of the Foundation of the
    American College of Healthcare Executives
1 North Franklin Street, Suite 1700
Chicago, IL 60606–3491
(312) 424–2800

Contents

Preface

There are four ways, and only four ways, in which we have contact with the world. We are evaluated and classified by these four contacts: what we do, how we look, what we say, and how we say it.

—Dale Carnegie

NOT LONG AGO I watched my young son maneuver his way through a maze of obstacles and challenges, strategically figuring out the best way to achieve mastery of one level so he could move to a higher one. Of course, he was playing a role-playing computer game.

I casually picked up the strategy guide beside him and thumbed through the pages. There in the index were interesting chapter headings such as "Building a Winning Party," "Know Thine Enemy," "Spells," and "Items." I began to see a distinct analogy between the strategic achievement of levels in this game of medieval knights and battles and the everyday strategies, tools, and tactics that are so necessary to healthcare organizations seeking to nurture their relationships with important constituencies.

I was intrigued by this comparison, so I examined another of his strategy guides. In the guide to one of his science fiction games I found these interesting chapters: "Tactical Systems," "Hints & Tips," "Walkthroughs," "Solutions," and "Officers." These guidelines, together with the ones in the previous book, reminded me of healthcare communication requirements such as strategies, alliances and audiences, tactics and tools, and simulations and plans.

I also considered the fact that the development of each of these aspects of a strategic communication program in healthcare has levels—levels that require mastery before being able to successfully maneuver through more complex scenarios. Just as in a computer game, learning how to maneuver your team successfully through a lower level provides you with considerable skill and knowledge to achieve your objectives when the situation is more complicated. The difference, however, lies in the fact that in our real-life situations, a higher level obstacle can pop up even before we're really ready. And while many managers consider communication to be a tool to achieve consensus (in other words, to persuade others to their way of thinking!), healthcare communication goes way beyond persuasion.

The result of this rumination is this book, *Beyond Persuasion: The Healthcare Manager's Guide to Strategic Communication.* My goal is to provide you with the knowledge, attitudes, and skills to use communication strategies and tactics to manage your organization's (and your own) relationships with important constituencies. Just as in a computer game, the player must be prepared to face real and potential challenges or obstacles, and then prevent or surmount these challenges. All of this is predicated on the idea that healthcare organizations need to consider their own self-interest, as well as the needs of the greater communities that they serve.

Dale Carnegie's admonition about the "only four ways" by which we are classified and evaluated by the world apply equally to healthcare organizations. In fact, organizational actions, as communicated through both behavior and words, become their public image or "look." And even neophyte public relations practitioners know that *perception is reality*. What people *believe* to be true is true for them in all its consequences, and they will act according to those beliefs. It is your job as a healthcare manager to ensure that what they believe about your organization is congruent with what you perceive is reality. Strategic communication through word and action is the way to accomplish this.

The bottom line is that strategic communication skills at the interpersonal, group, and organizational levels are crucially important for healthcare managers in today's world of communication overload. Whether conducting a meeting with employees, answering ever-increasing e-mail, or fielding reporters' questions at a press conference, both your own personal skills and how you use them in the overall strategic communication plan for your organization are important to your personal success, as well as to the success of your organization in achieving its mission.

Over the years I have observed that graduate programs in health administration are sadly lacking in course work on strategic communication as a management tool. Consequently, neophyte healthcare executives find themselves lacking fundamental concepts in how to best cultivate and use relationships with a variety of audiences, including the media. Indeed, healthcare executives whose educational background may be in business administration are essentially in the same situation. In any case, application of strategic communication concepts and practices is fundamentally an on-the-job problem.

HOW TO USE THIS BOOK

In a loose analogy to computer gaming, I have divided the material in this book into four levels, on the premise that the ideas in Level I are fundamental to those in Level II, and on up. Theoretically, mastery of the ideas, skills, tools, and tactics in one level should assist you in successfully achieving mastery at a higher level. However, as I mentioned earlier, challenges of a somewhat higher order often can and do emerge before you are really ready. Thus, the material in this book isn't entirely linear. The following figure illustrates what I mean about building strong foundations. (It might remind you a bit of first-year psychology and Abraham Maslow's Hierarchy of Needs.)

Level I provides an overview of professional foundations of communication in healthcare management as well as a detailed examination of the personal foundations needed—that is, your skills. This will allow you to consider and assess your own communication skills on a number of levels including both oral and written. Level II suggests that achieving communication goals begins close to home and that, in fact, neglect of this level leads to more problems at the following levels. Level III examines external communication, which is important in healthcare management. However, this discussion is not meant to be an exhaustive examination of all the external constituencies health-related organizations need to concern themselves with (for that

YOUR COMMUNICATION PYRAMID

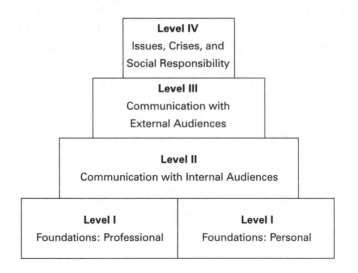

kind of a discussion, you will need to consult a textbook about public relations). Finally, Level IV broadens its view to examine crisis communication and the issue of social responsibility in healthcare communication.

Along the way, you will have an opportunity to figure out how you stack up in both your attitudes and your communication skills. In addition, at the end of each chapter you will find some guidance on where to look for further information—there are both books and Web resources to supplement this book's "quick and easy" approach.

Patricia Parsons

LEVEL I

Personal and Professional Foundations

The following five chapters introduce you to a variety of fundamental characteristics of healthcare communication in both the broad professional and the narrower personal venues.

The broad issues provide you with a working framework that we will use as our shared understanding and vocabulary to describe the concepts.

This section also allows you to take a very detailed look at your own communication skills. Together we will explore your attitudes and skills in interpersonal, written, and oral communication.

These concepts require mastery for full achievement of communication objectives as a manager and for the organization.

1
Communication as
a Management Tool

To the man who has only a hammer in his tool kit, every problem looks like a nail.

— Abraham Maslow

LET'S BEGIN WITH a peek at a day in the life of one healthcare manager.

*

By the time Michael Smith had a moment to even look at his watch, it was 9:20 a.m. He had already met with his senior managers about a pending labor dispute with their technical staff and sifted through 64 e-mail messages (64 messages!). He had answered the most urgent of them, taken a quick look at two departmental budgets, fielded a call from an irate board member whose daughter had not gotten the job she wanted on his staff, and now his secretary had just buzzed him to say that Carla MacDonald, his PR director, was waiting anxiously to see him. And he hadn't even had his coffee yet. *Such is the life of a hospital CEO,* he thought wryly.

Michael had been the CEO of St. Swithin's Health Sciences Center for almost five years and he actually liked his job despite

3

the fact that there were days like these when there seemed to be one problem after another. He knew Carla needed to discuss one of the most pressing with him.

St. Swithin's was caught between one of their most prestigious research scientists and a pharmaceutical company. The researcher had found that a drug she was testing on a group of patients did what the manufacturer said it would, but she had also found that it had significant deleterious—indeed life-threatening—side effects. She had discontinued using it and had gone public with her findings, in spite of an apparent gag order by the drug company, so that other researchers using the drug experimentally could protect their patients, too. The drug company was preparing to sue the doctor and St. Swithin's for breaching a confidentiality clause in the research grant contract. To make matters worse, the researcher and many of the other doctors at St. Swithin's were accusing the hospital of not standing behind its researchers and the ethical protection of patients. They were accusing hospital administration of bowing to the pressures of big business.

"Michael," Carla began, taking a seat in front of his desk and opening a large file folder full of papers. "We need to plan a press conference."

"Why can't we just send out releases? You know how much I hate facing the press."

Carla was adamant that they couldn't deal with all the hospital's relationship issues by sending out media releases and newsletters. Michael could write a dynamite memo or letter or e-mail message, and that was how he preferred to communicate. In fact, he was one of the few people he knew who had welcomed electronic communication with open arms—no longer would he be required to have small talk with anyone. It was a miracle. Carla, however, did not share his view.

She placed five press clippings on his desk. He had already seen three of them. He sighed and knew that he was going to have to listen to her.

*

Put yourself in Michael Smith's chair for a moment and consider how you would feel about his issues.

Abraham Maslow was the psychology luminary who pioneered the idea that people who are hungry, cold, or in physical pain are not likely to be interested in reaching for self-actualization. His work in understanding human behavior also indicated that people need a wide variety of skills to deal with the equally wide variety of challenges that come their way through life. Managers in healthcare facilities and organizations face ever more diverse issues on a daily basis, and their skill sets need to be eclectic as well. Communication issues, and the relationship problems and opportunities that arise from these issues, require managers with a high level of knowledge, an attitude that allows them to apply that knowledge in a strategic way, and highly developed skills that can be applied in diverse situations. The bottom line is that you need a variety of tools in your management tool kit, and communication skills are key to the successful application of most other tools and techniques of management.

THE MANAGER AS COMMUNICATOR

In 1955, the *Harvard Business Review* published a now-classic article (which they republished in 1974) that posed and answered the question: What observable skills does an effective executive demonstrate? The author divided the skills into technical, human, and conceptual, and indicated that the executive must be "skillful in communicating to others, in their own contexts, what he [sic] means by *his* [sic] behavior."[1] If we examine a healthcare manager's various functions and roles, we can develop a clear picture of where communication skills are key.

DEFINING MANAGEMENT

Management as a term is a bit like the word *personality*. Psychologists have difficulty defining it—there are as many definitions as there are psychologists studying it. The same is true of *manage-ment*. Most definitions, however, have some distinct commonal-ities.

First, management is a process of getting things done effi-ciently and effectively. It is not something that exists only at one point in time, but is continuous and dynamic, and in the process of "getting things done," specific outcomes can be measured.

Second, management accomplishes its goals through people as well as through the strategic use of other organizational re-sources, including time and money. What's crucial here is that people are key to a manager's ability to get things done.

Finally, most authors of basic texts in management agree that managers have four fundamental activities to use in the accomplishment of their goals: planning, organizing, leading, and controlling.[2]

Let's take a closer look at where communication plays a role in these aspects of management.

INTERPERSONAL SKILLS AND ROLES

If part of what a manager does is accomplish goals with and through people, little doubt exists that a manager must be a mas-ter communicator, first on an interpersonal level. Most people think they know what it means to have good interpersonal skills. They believe that an individual who appears to get along well with co-workers possesses these good skills. This is, however, an oversimplification when we're talking about a healthcare man-ager's skill set. A manager with good interpersonal skills is able to assess the situation in which the person-to-person interaction is taking place, understand the communication skill level of the other person, communicate his or her message clearly, listen well, and respond appropriately.

It is also true that managers play a variety of interpersonal roles, which might be described as the figurehead role, the leadership role, and the liaison role.³ As a *figurehead*, the health-care manager might speak at a conference of healthcare administration students, or hand out diplomas at the graduation ceremonies of the medical technology course hosted by his or her hospital.

In a *leadership* role, the manager is the one with the vision for the future of the organization, but also the responsibility to communicate that vision to the employees to ensure their buy-in and support for its accomplishment. This requires high-level interpersonal communication skills, as well as proficiency in the use of mediated communication (which will be discussed later).

The *liaison role* is played almost daily by managers at all levels in healthcare organizations. Henry Mintzberg, author of the now-classic text *The Nature of Managerial Work*, sees this liaison role as one of gathering information from sources external to the manager's own work unit.⁴ When the vice president of administrative services has a meeting with the transplant coordinators to gather information about how they are setting up flights to receive outside organ procurement teams, he or she is functioning in an internal liaison role. When the director of the transplant program meets with other such directors from other hospitals, this is an external liaison role. When the CEO meets with government representatives to discuss Medicare, this is also an external liaison.

Central to the success of each of these liaison encounters is the individual manager's communication skills at the interpersonal level. Interpersonal skills are important, but they aren't the only kind of communication skills that are crucial to the healthcare manager's success.

PROXIMITY

It might be a good time to consider the current issue of proximity when we examine interpersonal skills. Is it necessary to be in the same room with someone to use your interpersonal skills?

Not necessarily. Today's technological work environment often requires us to use mediated communication rather than direct, person-to-person communication. First, consider the telephone. You are not actually in the same room with the person with whom you are talking, and thus the communication values of such things as non-verbal cues are not available to you in interpreting what is being said or in conveying your own message. Your ability to communicate with that person on an interpersonal level, however, is still very important—it is just a bit different than if you were in the same room.

What about voice mail? Electronic mail? While good interpersonal skills might improve your ability to use these to their best advantage, they do require somewhat different skills. And while making a presentation at a large staff meeting might seem like an interpersonal approach, in fact it, too, requires a different set of skills again.

Here are some examples of where interpersonal skills are important in healthcare management:

- daily interaction with close staff
- interaction with medical staff
- interaction with individual board members
- negotiating with labor organizations
- interviewing staff and others
- disciplining staff
- being interviewed by media
- talking to patients and their families
- telephone calls
- internal or external meetings

WRITTEN COMMUNICATION

Healthcare managers also require a high level of achievement in the area of written communication. If we examine the managerial activities already mentioned (planning, organizing, leading, and controlling) it becomes clear that many of these require written communication for their successful accomplishment.

William Zinsser is arguably one of America's finest writing teachers. In his now-classic 1976 book *On Writing Well*, he lays it on the line by telling the reader this: "Few people realize how badly they write."[5] You may have graduated with a master's degree in health or business administration and written dozens of papers, perhaps even a thesis. You have written more exams than you care to remember and taken hundreds of pages of notes, but can you truly say that all of this makes you a good writer? If you didn't study applied communications at the college level, then it is likely that no one ever really taught you to write or evaluated your writing as a key part of the process. Writing, however, is fundamental to almost every other type of communication that is important in healthcare (or any other industry for that matter). Indeed, the roles and activities of managers, by their very nature, require excellence in written communication.

Here are some examples of where written communication skills are important in healthcare management:

- everyday e-mail
- letters to both internal and external individuals and groups
- correspondence with government
- speeches and presentations to employees, community groups, or government
- preparation for media interviews
- editing the written work of lower level staff
- your submission to the newsletter or annual report
- reports and proposals

Many basic textbooks on communicating within organizations seem to give short shrift to important aspects of written communication. Perhaps this is the reason why so many managers enter their positions believing that writing is something that they have already learned by osmosis. While writing requires a good grasp of the fundamentals of our language (spelling, punctuation, grammar, and syntax), it demands even more. Healthcare managers must be able to mold their writing to achieve specific and often diverse results, and must be able to target their writing to a variety of audiences including medical and non-medical staff, patients and their families, community groups, government, and the media. Writing academic papers in college is not necessarily good preparation for these challenges.

PRESENTATION SKILLS

The final skill set that is key to success in healthcare communication is presentation skills. This does not refer to chairing meetings, but rather to situations where you find yourself having to make an appearance before a group and be prepared to say something that is meaningful and targeted to that specific audience. Sometimes the group is interested in what you have to say—and sometimes it emphatically is not. Regardless of the reception, you have to be prepared and effective in front of your audience.

An oft-cited statistic claims that when Americans are polled about what they are most afraid of, public speaking ranks ahead of snakes, spiders, and even death. Therefore, it is likely that at least some healthcare managers are uncomfortable making presentations, and may even try to avoid every such situation. I believe that it is impossible to be a truly effective healthcare manager without highly developed presentation skills. Perhaps one of the most compelling reasons that some individuals fear public speaking is that their skill set is not at the level it should be.

Here are some examples of where presentation skills are important in healthcare management:

- facing the media at a press conference
- presenting the annual report to the board
- speaking to community groups
- acting as master of ceremonies at social functions
- conducting workshops for peers at conferences
- pitching to government or private groups for project support

Clearly communication skills are key to success as a health-care manager. Now is a good time to figure out what we really mean by the term *communication*.

COMMUNICATION IN THEORY AND PRACTICE

Just as the term *management* was difficult to define precisely, so too is the term *communication*. In fact, the author of one book on communication theory lists 126 such attempts![6] Some of the definitions refer specifically to verbal communication, while others are broader. Some focus on the goals of communication while others focus on the medium. While all of this is useful for a prolonged discussion of the semantics of the issue, we need a clear definition of healthcare communication upon which we can all agree. For the purposes of this book, we will define it as follows:

Healthcare communication is a two-way process of informing, persuading, and sharing ideas using the most appropriate medium for the situation and for the participants.

It is crucially important to recognize that while the purpose of much of your communication activity on a daily basis might appear to be one-way (e-mail, letters, and meetings), the reality is that there needs to be an opportunity for a two-way process within every communication encounter. The reason for this is that communication is the foundation upon which relationships are built (more about this in the next section). Even a small e-mail message designed to provide the receivers with specific information needs to be open to feedback.

The simplest model of communication in healthcare is illustrated in Figure 1.1. The healthcare manager is the sender of the message, the receiver picks up that message, and a feedback loop allows the manager to know of the receiver's response. Did the receiver actually receive the message? Did the receiver understand the message? Does the receiver have anything to add to the message? Does the receiver agree/disagree with the message? The answers to all of these questions are useful information for the manager. The manager who ignores this aspect of the communication process does so at his or her peril!

COMMUNICATION AND RELATIONSHIP BUILDING

If we look more critically at the simple communication model in Figure 1.1, we find that it doesn't really provide any indication of why we might communicate. Initially, we might consider that communication is required to inform and to persuade. If we examine this more closely, it is clear that communication theorists

FIGURE 1.1   A MODEL OF COMMUNICATION

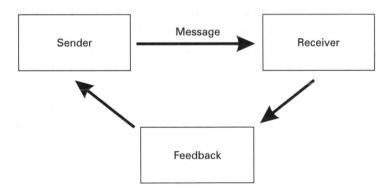

aren't too far off base when they tell us that we communicate to fulfill a human need. (Indeed, a number of telecommunication companies have based their advertising campaigns on this concept.) While all of this is useful when we are talking about communication within our own personal worlds, are the same reasons sufficient to support the need to be a highly skilled communicator in your job in healthcare? Not really.

In the context of your job as a healthcare manager, one of the most important reasons to consider the quality of your communication is because the relationships that you have with other individuals—and that your organization has with other groups and organizations—often originate directly from the quality of the communication that has flowed between you and these others.

If we go back to the scenario played out at the beginning of this chapter, we find Michael Smith in a situation that has implications for his own and his hospital's relationships with a variety of individuals and groups. If Michael is a master communicator and has placed a high value on his communication over the past four years, it will be much easier for him to deal with the current situation.

- If Michael has cultivated a good interpersonal relationship with the director of the medical staff, that individual will feel comfortable going directly to Michael to discuss the current situation with the researcher. It is then less likely that the medical staff members who are concerned about the hospital's commitment to, and support of, their research will discuss the situation with the media before administration knows about it.
- If Michael has been strategic about his communication efforts with the medical staff as a group, the positive relationship would make it less likely for them to jump to

conclusions about how senior administration is handling this situation.

- If Michael has been strategic about his communication with his hospital board and has maintained a policy of keeping them informed, there is less likelihood that any board members will feel that they have to enter into the fray without first allowing senior administration to have their say.
- If Michael has been an effective spokesperson when members of the media have asked to interview him from time to time over the years, they are more likely to provide his hospital's senior administration with a fair hearing and airing in the media.
- If Michael has been a solid member of the community, supporting community issues and events, providing his leadership and expertise when necessary—developed a good relationship—they will cut him more slack before forming their own opinions of the hospital's behavior.

These are just a few of the crucial long-term relationships that can have either a positive or negative effect on both the day-to-day activities of a healthcare organization and on crisis situations. While it may seem at first glance that it is the organization's relationship, rather than the manager's, with these groups that is most crucial, the CEO's own personal communication skills and knowledge will play a key part. At lower levels in the organizational hierarchy, the situation for managers is similar. In this particular situation, the director of pharmaceutical services may find him or herself on the firing line. This individual's strategic communication skills will also play a role in the direction of the outcome, positive or negative.

PUBLIC RELATIONS

Before we go any further, we need to understand another term and another role within your organization. That is the public relations (PR) function in healthcare and how your own mastery of strategic communication plays a role in that managerial area.

Public relations uses communications tools and techniques to help organizations develop and maintain relationships.[7] What this means to you is that your public relations department (if you don't have one, we'll get to that) should be expected to have expertise in all areas of strategic communication for the purposes of assisting your organization to achieve the good will of important publics both internally and externally. Furthermore, you should be able to rely on them for expert advice in the development of your own skills, whether you are the CEO or a manager at a lower level. If, however, you are a manager in a small organization that does not have a PR staff, then you probably have an even more crucially important role in strategic communications. (We will go into more detail about this in Chapter 8.)

The bottom line is that in your role as a manager in a healthcare facility or health-related organization, every communication encounter that you personally have with any person or group inside or outside your working environment will have an effect on both your and the organization's relationship with a variety of constituencies. And the good will of these groups could be key to the accomplishment of your mission.

WHO THE MANAGER
COMMUNICATES WITH

Healthcare managers communicate with a wide variety of people and groups on a daily basis. Some of these encounters are planned, while others simply spring up during the course of the day's work. If you were to make a list of the number of communication encounters you have in the run of a working day, how many could you come up with? Here are the important groups with whom you communicate. Most of the people and groups on your own list should fit into one of these general classifications:

- employees
- medical staff
- board members
- financial donors/potential financial donors
- patients and their families
- potential patients and their families
- community members
- financial institutions
- government
- the media
- community health–related organizations
- regulatory bodies and professional organizations
- suppliers

You probably noted already that these broad groupings could be broken down even more finely, but for now this general list allows us to consider the implications of the encounters.

Each of these groups has a different reason for wanting to communicate with you, and you have a different objective for every communication encounter you initiate. The question is: Are you ready to communicate effectively with each of these groups to achieve your own strategic objectives for yourself and your organization? By the end of the next few chapters, you should be able to answer that question more accurately.

KEY POINTS

1. Communication is a crucial leadership tool for success in healthcare management.

2. Communication skills at the interpersonal level are important in managerial roles, including the leadership role, the figurehead role, and the liaison role.

3. Written communication skills are fundamental to almost all aspects of healthcare management, including strategic planning, relationship building, and organizational development.

4. Highly developed presentation skills are often the key difference between the manager and the leader.

5. Open, two-way communication is the desired model in healthcare management.

6. An understanding of the public relations function in healthcare provides the manager with a broader basis for being strategic in his or her communication encounters.

NOTES
1. Katz, R. 1974. "Skills of an Effective Administrator." *Harvard Business Review* (September-October): p. 91.
2. Parsons, P. J. 2000. *A Manager's Guide to P.R. Projects.* Halifax, NS: Biomedical Communications, Inc.
3. Robbins, S. P., M. Coulter, and R. Stuart-Kotze. 1997. *Management.* Scarborough, Ontario: Prentice Hall Canada, Inc.
4. Mintzberg, H. 1973. *The Nature of Managerial Work.* New York: Harper and Row.
5. Zinsser, W. 1980. *On Writing Well: An Informal Guide to Writing Non-Fiction.* New York: Harper & Row, p. 19.
6. Dance, F. E. and C. E. Larson. 1976. *The Functions of Human Communication.* New York: Hold, Rinehart, and Winston, Appendix A.
7. Parsons, op. cit.

FOR YOUR BOOKSHELF . . .

Cutlip, Scott M., Allen H. Center, and Glen M. Broom. 2000. *Effective Public Relations.* 8th ed. Prentice Hall.

Hamilton, Cheryl. 1997. *Communicating for Results: A Guide for Business and the Professions.* 5th ed. Wadsworth Publishing Company.

Parsons, Patricia J. 2000. *The Manager's Guide to* PR *Projects.* Biomedical Communications Inc.

ON THE WEB . . .

Corporate Culture
http://www.auxillium.com/culture.htm

Growing the Corporate Culture
http://www.smartbiz.com/sbs/arts/ste9.htm

The Strategic Process

The plan is nothing. Planning is everything!

— Dwight D. Eisenhower

ANY MANAGER WORTH his or her salt already knows a great deal about being strategic. However, as healthcare management consultant Alan Zuckerman points out, "Failure to *implement* [emphasis added] a strategic plan is one of the most common flaws of the strategic planning process."[1]

When it comes to communication by healthcare managers, not only is the plan not implemented, but it is often neglected entirely. For many managers, communication is simply something that they do every day, giving it little thought and even less strategic consideration. Before we move into our discussion of communication as a strategic process, let's look in on Michael Smith, our hospital CEO, and his PR director.

*

"Okay, Carla," Michael said, reading one of the press clippings in front of him on his desk. "We'll have a press conference."

"It isn't quite that simple," Carla said as she gathered the clippings and slipped them into her portfolio.

Michael sighed. Nothing ever was.

"Everything we say to the press has implications for a lot of other people and groups."

"I suppose you mean the medical staff?" Michael said.

"That's only the beginning." Carla pulled another sheaf of papers out and began to lay them on the desk. There were figures with circles and arrows, charts, tables, and pages of narrative.

Step by step Carla took Michael through her thoughts about what she called a domino effect. She explained to him that whatever he and the rest of the hospital said to anyone about the problem with the pharmaceutical company would have an effect on any number of other individuals and groups. She explained that there might even be groups that hadn't formed yet or that they hadn't thought about yet.

For example, in their midst they had nurse-researchers from the university whose response would have to be considered. All employees would be concerned if they thought that the hospital wouldn't even stand behind their high-profile, apparently highly prized researchers. Where would that leave them? Then, of course, there were the citizen groups who were concerned with the safety of clinical trials of new drugs.

The bottom line was that before they did anything, they would have to know the answers to a number of key questions:

- What were they doing about the situation?
- What were they prepared to say?
- How would they say it?
- To whom would they say it and how would the message have to be tailored to fit the interests and concerns of each group?
- What method would they use to get the message to the important groups?
- Who would be the messenger for each group?
- When would each of the groups receive their message?

- How would they know that the message was received accurately?
- How would they gauge the overall response to their approach?

Carla and Michael together determined that above all they needed to safeguard the good reputation of their hospital, but that their own mission and philosophy determined that they had to be as honest as they could with their important constituencies without jeopardizing anyone's right to privacy. That included the privacy of both patients and staff members. With the answers to these questions and a values-based framework, they were on solid ground to move forward to accomplish their goal.

*

"We need a plan!"

How often have you heard someone say this, or even said it yourself? Webster's dictionary defines plan as "an arrangement of means or steps for the attainment of some object; a scheme; method; design . . . a model of action."[2] So, what you are really saying is that you need an *intention* to do something. Having a plan is a good thing, but simply having a plan does not by its mere existence mean that anything will be done with it.

While planning as an exercise may be important, the process of implementation in healthcare communication planning is key. Thus, we need to consider communication planning as a *process*, a term that is defined more as a "forward movement."[3] This concept of movement is crucial.

SEAT-OF-THE-PANTS COMMUNICATIONS

"We better call in PR!"

When do you usually hear this cry for help? Before a problem has occurred? Or does it seem more common that this phrase is heard when a problem has arisen and some relationship needs patching?

For too many years, healthcare organizations took many of their important relationships that were built on communication processes for granted. Thus, communication became more of a fire-fighting, rather than a fire-preventing, process:

- We won't bother to develop a dialogue with our nursing staff until they threaten to go on strike.
- We don't need to initiate contact with the government until they threaten our Medicare payments.
- I don't need to give any thought to how I answer my e-mail—until someone feels he or she has been slighted.

Many problems that organizations face with their relationships are a direct result of dealing with communication issues in a reactive, rather than a proactive, way.

STRATEGIC STEPS AND THE DOMINO EFFECT

To take a proactive approach to your communication as a healthcare manager means that you will consciously choose to see each communication encounter as a four-step process. Just as in any other strategic planning situation, there are clearly defined steps that you can use as a framework for thinking about the process, keeping in mind that the reality of individual situations can be considerably messier. This proactive approach, however, can reduce this sloppiness and unpredictability considerably.

The key questions delineated in our scenario offer a starting point for determining the four steps: research, plan, implement, and evaluate.

RESEARCH

The first step is, of course, research. Most strategic planners call this a situational analysis. But research is a broader term that encompasses the simplest to the most complex communication challenges. The amount of data-gathering and analysis that you will need to do varies widely in communication situations.

For example, as a healthcare manager, you face every day what you might be tempted to refer to as routine correspondence, whether it comes via the postal service, your e-mail account, or even voice mail. Most managers have devised ways of dealing with such routine communication and, luckily, these routine approaches often have good results. Sometimes, however, the results are less productive than they could be, or even cause further problems of which you may not be aware. I am not suggesting that you need to embark on a complicated research process for every piece of correspondence that you have to deal with, but what is required is an internalized process for quickly gathering and analyzing the information you need. Here are the questions that should be in your mind as you deal with any communication situation:

- Who is this person/organization?
- What is this person/organization's relationship to me and/or my organization?
- What other persons/organizations have relevant relationships?
- How important is the issue? How important could the issue become?

The answers to these questions will provide a basis for dealing with everything from e-mail questions from potential clients/patients to a phone call from a reporter after allegations of staff misconduct. You should also be able to see where the issue of the so-called domino effect is beginning to emerge. You are not simply communicating with a particular individual or organization, but potentially with a whole host of others who might be affected by how you deal with the situation.

PLAN

After you have established the basics, you need a plan of attack for dealing with the challenge, regardless of how simple or complex it might be. Whether you need a written plan or just the one in your head depends on a number of factors including the complexity of the situation, the extent of its potential ramifications, and your own skills in using the particular communication mode.

Generally, the more complex the situation and the greater the significance of the outcomes, the greater the need for a written plan to which you can refer at a later date if necessary. Most important to consider, however, is the state of your own communication skills using different modalities (we'll examine those in detail in the next few chapters). For example, if you believe that your writing skills could use some work (or someone has pointed this out to you), then you probably need to begin to outline your work before you write even a simple e-mail. This outline is your plan. If your interpersonal skills are your weak link, you need a written plan prior to meetings. Everyone needs a written plan prior to making a public presentation whether at the chamber of commerce luncheon or at a press conference.

The plan, however, needn't be too complex. In fact, the simpler the better. All it really needs to include are:

- a few considerations about who this person/organization is,
- what you would like to accomplish,
- a clear statement of your message, and
- thoughts about the best medium to convey this message.

If we focus on the last point about medium, it may be worth considering a few issues. If the message came to you by mail, perhaps what you really need to do now is make a phone call or set up a meeting. If you are having a meeting, you may also need to prepare a written document that will convey your message.

IMPLEMENT

After you have considered your plan, the next step is to implement it. Implementing communication in healthcare involves your own personal set of skills in the areas of interpersonal communication, written communication, and public presentation. We will discuss these in some detail in the chapters to come.

EVALUATE

Finally, you need to evaluate the outcomes of your communication. As you are sending that e-mail, handing your assistant the tape of correspondence, or stepping down from the podium, you should think about how you will know if this has had the effect you intended. Communication doesn't end when the deliberate part of the process is over.

COMMUNICATION AND YOUR MISSION STATEMENT

Sometimes what you would like to say or write to someone is not really what is promoted in your organization's mission, philosophy, and values. Therefore, rather than thinking about how this hampers your ability to communicate in the way you see fit, your organization's mission is better viewed as a kind of blueprint for the tone and direction of your communication processes.

Different kinds of health-related organizations have different kinds of missions. While issues of caring and curing may be part of many, this by no means represents the whole of what healthcare organizations do. We will look at some examples of mission statements to see how these might help in the strategic approach to healthcare communication.

First, examine the following missions of several large, tertiary care institutions. While there are similarities, as one would expect, they are not all exactly the same. Therefore, the relationships that they define vary slightly, setting different tones for their communication processes.

Mission Statement 1

To provide the highest quality care to individuals and to the community, to advance care through excellence in biomedical research, and to educate future academic and practice leaders of the health care professions.

— *Massachusetts General Hospital*

Massachusetts General Hospital[4] is clear about the importance not only of individual patients, but also about the position of the community. In addition, research and education, which are to be expected of tertiary care facilities, are also clearly stated in the mission. These are aspects of what they do that need to be front and center in making decisions about how managers will communicate with both internal and external audiences.

Mission Statement 2

[We are] a health care community dedicated to improving the health of children. Our mission is to provide the best in family-centred [sic], compassionate care, to lead in scientific and clinical advancement, and to prepare the next generation of leaders in child health.

— *Hospital for Sick Children, Toronto*

The Hospital for Sick Children[5] in Toronto, Canada, is also a tertiary care facility, but one with a narrower patient population. Their mission clearly states that families are very important.

Mission Statement 3

Our mission is to find cures for children with catastrophic illnesses through research and treatment.

—*St. Jude Children's Research Hospital, Memphis*

St. Jude Children's Research Hospital,[6] while providing care for a similar patient population as the Hospital for Sick Children in Toronto, has a slightly more focused mission that points directly to its role in finding cures for childhood diseases.

As we move from tertiary care facilities to examine the mission statements of smaller hospitals, Griffin Hospital[7] in Connecticut (a 160-bed, acute care community hospital) provides a good example of a communication approach that needs quite a different tone than the previous ones. The references to consumers and empowerment are clear and will direct the nature of effective communication from a facility such as this one, and from its managers.

Mission Statement 4

Griffin Hospital is committed to providing personalized, humanistic, consumer-driven health care in a healing environment, to empowering individuals to be actively involved in decisions affecting their care and well-being through access to information and education, and to providing leadership to improve the health of the community we serve.

—*Griffin Hospital, Derby, Connecticut*

If we examine the missions of two different kinds of health-related organizations, it becomes even clearer how to use the organizational mission statement as a guide in the strategic process of healthcare communications.

Mission Statement 5

As a retirement-assisted living and convalescent care organization, we are dedicated to promoting the well-being of our residents. We recognize and respect each individual's rights, needs and circumstances and strive to promote a supportive community that nurtures the body, mind and spirit.

—Cascade Vista, Redmond, Washington

A long-term care facility, Cascade Vista[8] is not focused on research and cures, but clearly on nurturing. The messages regarding both the type of services provided and to whom the services are provided are apparent in all of the above mission statements—all clear bases for both personal and organizational communication efforts.

The next mission statement is representative of a different kind of health-related organization and its message also provides tone and direction.

Mission Statement 6

The American Occupational Therapy Association advances the quality, availability, use, and support of occupational therapy through standard-setting, advocacy, education, and research on behalf of its members and the public.

— American Occupational Therapy Association

A membership organization such as the American Occupational Therapy Association[9] speaks to a different primary audience than do the mission statements of healthcare facilities. As a health-related organization that represents health professionals, their contract with society as documented in their mission statement describes a different kind of relationship, and therefore will require a different approach to communication.

The organizational mission statement assists us in the development of a strategic approach to communication in a number of ways.

First, when they are written well, mission statements provide a good understanding of the most important audiences with whom a manager will be required to communicate. Although they clearly don't provide an exhaustive list of constituencies, they do set the priority, provided the mission is a working document and not a pretty picture to hang on the lobby wall.

Second, mission statements set the priority for what an organization does. Often this can be useful when dealing with a communication issue that seeks to have the organization carry out a role for which it is not suited.

Finally, and most important from a communication perspective, the mission statement sets the tone for communication and even provides a certain level of vocabulary. If the tone set by the mission is not what the organization sees as appropriate, the mission statement needs revision.

If you examine your own organizational mission statement, what kinds of words do you see? If you have never looked at the mission from this perspective before, some of the words may lend themselves to your own communication efforts by setting the tone and providing some inspiration when you are searching for the right words:

quality	empowering
excellence	community
future	respect
compassionate	advance
leadership	enhance
personalized	image
humanistic	rights

COMMUNICATION AND CORPORATE CULTURE IN HEALTHCARE

Although organizations have clearly had "personalities" since people began organizing, the term "corporate culture" has only actually been a part of our vocabularies since the early 1980s. Since that time, among both academics and managers, interest has increased in attempting to understand the organizational behaviors that go beyond those that are most easily explained by either economics or logic. The study of corporate culture has been the result of this rumination, and organizational mission statements, with their tone and direction, lead to the question of how this cultural phenomenon might relate to managerial communication.

In their book *We Mean Business: Building Communication Competence in Business and Professions,* authors William Gorden and Randi Nevins explain that "employees' job satisfaction and organizational commitment hinge upon whether they share beliefs within the culture."[10] Indeed, the extent to which organizations, including both not-for-profit and for-profit, are able to achieve their missions, depends largely on how they are able to communicate this vision to their employees and eventually to their important external audiences. What is interesting here is that an organization's communication is both a product of the type of culture it exhibits as well as a creator of that culture. Thus, your own communication style as a manager is having a direct effect on the communication climate in your department or institution, the culture that showcases that climate, and ultimately the extent to which you are able to assist your organization to achieve its objectives. This simple logic underlines the importance of one manager's communication skills and attitudes.

OBSTACLES TO COMMUNICATION

Communication plans often go awry and fail to accomplish even the most modest objectives for the communication encounter.

There can be any number of reasons for even the best-laid plans to falter. One of the most glaring is the failure to take into account the potential obstacles when planning what we intend to say and how we intend to say it.

One way to categorize these obstacles is to identify those that are related to the sender of the message, as well as those that are a function of the receiver. Perhaps a more useful way to think about these, however, is to make a checklist for examining a failed communication encounter. When you are examining the fall-out from an unsuccessful communication effort—whether it is a meeting that didn't meet the mark, a presentation that seemed to not be well-received, or a newspaper article that has misinterpreted your statements—the answers to the following questions may help you to pinpoint the obstacle that you failed to consider at the outset.

COMMUNICATION OBSTACLE CHECKLIST

- Do I respect both the audience and the medium?
- Was I anxious about any aspect of the encounter?
- Are my own skills in this kind of situation as sharp as they should be?
- Was I well enough prepared for this communication encounter?
- Did I have enough information about my audience?
- Does this audience respect me and/or the organization I represent?
- Does this audience have a sufficient level of interest in this subject?
- Does this audience possess the skills necessary to use the medium I selected?
- Does this audience have access to the medium I chose?

If you answered "no" to any of the questions on the checklist, you may want to explore that issue more. If you answer "no" to the same question in a number of unsuccessful communication situations, you have probably pinpointed one of your own personal issues with communication.

CARVED IN STONE?

A strategic plan for communication — whether for a large-scale organizational effort or a personal daily communication encounter — must be dynamic. A static plan, which looks good on paper but is not subject to change, fails to recognize that situations can and do change. As you gather more information, you may need to alter aspects of your approach for any of the following reasons:

- You may need to change your message if new information has altered the sense of what you are saying.
- You may need to change how the message is worded if new knowledge about your audience will affect your message.
- You may need to select another medium if the chosen one is inaccessible, too expensive (either for you or your audience), or of little interest to your audience.

These are some examples of modifications that may need to be made. As you consider changes to your plan of attack for a communication encounter, you create concrete data upon which to build the next approach.

KEY POINTS

1. Healthcare managers should realize that to be effective, communication at all levels needs to be the result of a strategic process.

2. Many organizations experiencing problems in their relationships with both internal and external groups may be using reactive rather than proactive communication strategies.

3. Each communication approach should be the result of having collected enough data from which the plan of attack was developed.

4. Each communication encounter requires an evaluation at some level.

5. Organizational mission statements provide clues to strategic communication by indicating both underlying message and tone.

6. Managerial communication in healthcare organizations contributes to the development of a culture that supports goal achievement or lack of achievement.

7. Strategic approaches to communication encounters need to be flexible and subject to change as a result of feedback.

NOTES

1. Zuckerman, A. M. 1998. *Healthcare Strategic Planning: Approaches for the 21ˢᵗ Century*. Chicago: Health Administration Press, p. 10.

2. *New Illustrated Webster's Dictionary of the English Language*. 1992. New York: PMC Publishing Company, Inc., p. 742.

3. *Webster's, op cit.*, p. 772.

4. Http://www.mgh.harvard.edu/about/mission.htm

5. Http://www.sickkids.on.ca/about/mission.asp

6. Http://www.stjude.org/sr/mission.htm

7. Http://www.griffinhealth.org/about/mission.html

8. Http://www.cascadevista.com/mission&background.htm

9. Http://www.aota.org/about.asp

10. Gorden, W. and R. Nevins. 1993. *We Mean Business: Building Communication Competence in Business and Professions*. New York: Harper Collins College Publishers, p. 14.

FOR YOUR BOOKSHELF . . .

Ferguson, Sherry Devereaux. 1999. *Communication Planning: An Integrated Approach*. Sage.

3 Interpersonal Skills

We are what we repeatedly do; excellence, then, is no
act, but a habit.

— Aristotle

WHAT DO YOUR own personal habits say about you as a communicator? What do they say about you as a representative of your organization or of your industry? How much do you rely on the communication skills of others without giving a lot of thought to your own skills? In short, how do *you* stack up?

In this chapter, we will begin our exploration of your skills as a communicator by examining important aspects of interpersonal communication and some healthcare management situations where these person-to-person skills are key. By the end of the chapter, you should have increased insight into your own level of skills in this area.

A PERSONAL THING

Defining *interpersonal communication* as a concept has become more difficult as communication technology has become more complex, yet at the same time, more accessible. Many communication theorists believe that this dyadic form of communication isn't really all that different from other levels of communication (i.e., group, organizational, and mass communication). In fact, if you examine these levels closely, it seems clear that there are elements of the interpersonal in each of them.[1] For example, whenever you attend or chair a group meeting, your one-on-one skills are very important. When you are being interviewed by a newspaper reporter, although your message will ultimately end up in the mass media, there is little doubt that your own interpersonal skills will be an important factor in your success at using the reporter as the conduit through which your message must initially pass.

So, while purists might consider interpersonal communication as an in-person, dyadic encounter, the skills you display in this kind of situation will clearly enhance or detract from your abilities in a much wider variety of communication situations.

Three important elements affect any situation in which you must communicate with another person on an interpersonal level: your relationship with that other person, the two communicators (the receiver is also a communicator), and the dialogue itself. Let's begin by examining the relationship between you and your partner in communication.

UP, DOWN, AND ACROSS

It is very difficult for anyone in our society to spend much time without facing situations requiring interpersonal communication—and it is impossible for healthcare managers to do their jobs without it, regardless of their level in the hierarchy. Approaches to communicating in this one-on-one fashion, however, differ depending upon both the formal and informal relationship you have with the receiver of your messages.

One way to consider the formal relationships that provide a framework for your interpersonal encounters is to examine a formal reporting structure such as your organizational chart. Your interpersonal communication differs in a variety of ways depending upon your formal relationship with the other person. Figure 3.1 is an example of a typical hierarchical organizational chart. The objectives, tone, message, and potential outcomes will vary considerably; it is important not to disregard them.

For example, if you are communicating with employees over whom you have authority, this will color the encounter. How they perceive your management style will provide the backdrop against which they will interpret your messages, for better or for worse. In the end, however, you will inevitably be interpreted in the context of your authority.

On the other hand, when you are communicating with those on your own level, even if they personally feel either above you or below you (in terms of expertise), they know that they are your peers. A formal lateral relationship is different than a vertical one.

Then, of course, there is the informal relationship. These informal relationships can be a result of a variety of conditions, including:

- pre-existing relationships (such as a family tie or a college roommate);

FIGURE 3.1   THE ORGANIZATIONAL CHART FOR PUBLIC CONSUMPTION

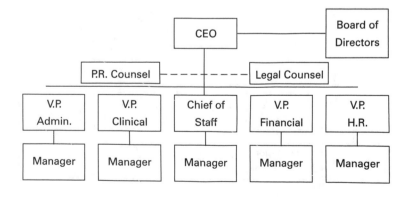

- current social interactions;
- your pre-conceived notions of someone else's relationships; or
- your pre-conceived opinions about someone's expertise.

Now compare the organizational chart in Figure 3.2 to the previous one. You can see that the hidden parts of the chart can have considerable influence in the tone, style, content, and direction of communication.

Unfortunately, using an organizational chart is not useful at all when you consider your relationship with people outside your organization. They, however, will also judge your message based on where they believe you sit: above them, below them, or on the same level. The criteria that individuals may use to determine your relative level include perceived expertise, perceived experience, age, gender, educational level, and sometimes even race, as much as we like to consider that we've evolved beyond this. On the other hand, these are the same criteria by which you subconsciously determine where others sit in relation to you as well. The bottom line is that the better you really know the person with whom you are interacting, and the more accurately they perceive you, the fewer obstacles you will encounter in the

FIGURE 3.2   THE ORGANIZATIONAL CHART (AS IT REALLY WORKS)

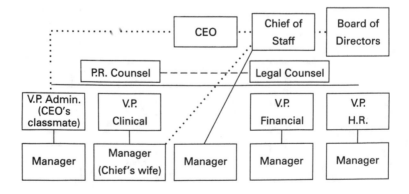

interpersonal exchange. The important lesson here is that even when you are communicating in a simple dyadic structure, you still need as much information about your audience as possible.

THE GOOD, THE BAD, AND THE NEUTRAL

Not only do you have to consider horizontal and vertical relationships, you will also need to examine closely the quality of the relationship that you have with others.

If you have a long-standing, positive, productive relationship with someone—which is your goal—you will have little difficulty developing a rapport, even in situations where you might find yourself on opposite sides of an argument. This implies that every encounter you have with any individual will have potential consequences on the kind of communication that you can affect when the need arises. A person with whom you have a positive relationship will cut you more slack when the going gets tough.

On the other hand, you may have cultivated negative relationships (or in fact failed to cultivate a relationship at all). A negative relationship is often characterized by an apparent lack of common ground. It can develop insidiously as you inadvertently deal with individuals without giving overt consideration to the long-term consequences of each encounter that you have. A negative relationship has a significant effect on the way each encounter is perceived. Often, the attitudes are unfavorable from the outset, regardless of the topic under discussion. This kind of an interpersonal relationship can make achieving goals much more difficult and time-consuming than necessary. If you take a few minutes to consider the individuals with whom you have personally negative relationships, you will recognize that if the relationship itself were improved, finding common ground and a positive starting point would be much easier.

Finally, you probably have a great number of encounters where you either have no relationship or a relationship that you can only classify as neutral. This is at least preferable to the negative relationship. Sometimes, it is to your advantage to maintain your neutral relationships, but you will encounter many individuals with whom it would be to your benefit to proactively cultivate a positive one.

MYTHS ABOUT INTERPERSONAL COMMUNICATION

Your beliefs about communication in general and your own skills in particular have an enormous effect on your success or failure as a communicator. Here are some commonly held beliefs that are, in fact, myths.

1. *People pay attention when you speak to them.* Unless the other person is really interested in what you are saying (this means they have a personal stake in it), he or she is likely not really paying attention at all and certainly not to the extent that you may believe. One telling piece of trivia: a human being is said to absorb 600 to 1200 words per minute when, on average, we speak at about 150 words per minute. If you do the math you realize that the listener has time to fill in the gaps with his or her own thoughts, rather than giving you their full attention. Do you always pay attention when someone else is talking to you? Or do you occasionally think about your next meeting, your grocery list, or your child's report card?

2. *If you think something is important, others will, too.* This could not be more untrue. You have to be able to express how the issue affects the other person and have that other person buy into it. This takes more than your enthusiasm (or anger, outrage, or intensity). It takes a good deal of researching in advance to determine how the other person might actually

be interested in the issue, then creating your message to begin on common ground.

3. *When people nod their heads in agreement, they really have understood and agreed with you.* Wrong again. Nodding means nothing. A nod is no more or less than a gesture of acknowledgment that you are saying something—what that something is may or may not be understood. Further, the listener is showing neither agreement or disagreement.

4. *When people say they understand what you have said, they do.* More frequently, that person will go away and begin to think about what you have said (if it is important enough to think about). Once away from you, the other person will find many other factors that will have an effect on what you have said and you won't be there to address them.

5. *Repeating yourself is a good way to ensure that the listener understands.* Wrong. Saying something over and over, even using different words, is a very common and ineffective way to get your message across. Parents do it all the time, and so do bosses.

6. *Using emotional outbursts, including saying something more loudly, ensures that the listener receives your message.* If the listener did not understand what you were trying to say when you said it in a more modulated tone, speaking loudly or getting overly emotional will negatively affect your relationship and how the other person perceives your message.

7. *Using extreme gestures will get your point across better.* Pounding your fist on the table is a good example of this kind of gesture. It has the same effect as yelling (see item 6), which means that it can be perceived negatively and turn the listener against your message.

As you climb the ladder of managerial success, you might think that your position affords you some kind of special situation regarding these myths. Your subordinates may be forced into situations where you are attempting to communicate with them, but if you haven't taken the time to cultivate more positive relationships, they are no more likely to receive your messages than if you were on the same level as they are.

CULTIVATING POSITIVE RELATIONSHIPS

How do you cultivate a positive relationship with another person with whom it is imperative that you communicate? Let's begin with a quick inventory of your own communication style. Look at the checklist in Figure 3.3. Check off as many of these behaviors as you believe you have ever exhibited in the specified interpersonal encounters.

If you check off even one, think carefully about whether that exhibition was a one-time incident, or a pattern of behavior. If you find yourself checking off *any* of these behaviors, you probably

FIGURE 3.3   BEHAVIORAL CHECKLIST

Behavior	In person	On the phone	At a meeting
yelling			
finger pointing			
making digs or jokes			
crying or whining			
being condescending			
refusing to respond			
interrupting or over-talking			

realize that they are not conducive to successful interpersonal communication.

You may believe that yelling and pointing fingers (or pounding on the desk) are necessary in some situations, but they are not. This is an aggressive display that fails to lead to the kind of rapport that will allow you to meet your strategic goals. Whining and crying can be perceived as passive-aggressive behavior, while condescension is not high on the list of ways to win support either. Refusing to respond makes you resemble a stone wall, while interrupting and over-talking can signal a number of underlying issues such as self-centeredness, not listening, or simple rudeness.

If any of these are part of your interpersonal toolbox, you need to take a good, hard look at your relationships with other people. In addition, you may notice that you are more likely to exhibit a certain kind of negative behavior in a specific kind of situation. This will need to be monitored so that you can replace the negative behaviors with more positive ones. There is an old proverb that may help you to begin this process: "I not only speak so that I can be understood, but so that I cannot be misunderstood."

Negative interpersonal behavior contributes to unintended messages that may lead people to misunderstand your message and your motives.

YOUR MEETING STYLE

Do you have to go to a meeting today? Do you have to chair a meeting? Welcome to the wonderful world of management! Interpersonal communication skills are key to your potential for attaining strategic goals through meetings. The question is, what kind of interpersonal style comes through when you are participating in a meeting?

Generally, the positive interpersonal behavior that we have been discussing is a good basis for achieving your objectives in the context of a meeting as well. Meetings, however, have their own set of rules, and what is acceptable in some interpersonal situations may not be acceptable at a meeting (or vice versa).

In his book *Effective Meetings: The Complete Guide*, author Clyde Burleson provides us with a fundamental guideline: "All present in a meeting are equals insofar as their making a contribution to that meeting."[2] He is referring specifically to the fact that everyone has the equal right to express their views, have opinions, and even to vote. Keeping this in mind may help to focus your behavior and your responses appropriately.

Acceptable behavior at meetings varies considerably from one industry to another, but healthcare tends to be somewhat more conservative than, for example, the advertising business. In addition, meetings with various groups have their own dynamics and their own codes of conduct. For example, a meeting of the medical staff is likely to have different dynamics than a meeting of managers. Factors that can affect these meetings are such things as how well the participants know each other, the extent to which they share similar backgrounds and an understanding of the issues being discussed, and the history of how well this group may have worked together in the past.

If you are a manager attending a meeting of a group of health professionals whose backgrounds you don't share, the way you are viewed by that group will affect the dynamics. For example, if you are an administrator and are attending a meeting of the medical staff, your presence may change the usual group dynamics, perhaps injecting a degree of formality that may not normally be there. Indeed, your relationship with individual members of the group, the direct result of your interpersonal skills, will be the biggest factor.

In general, meetings in which most of the participants know each other well tend to have a more personal style. However, this personal style may be disturbed by a guest. When this happens, all participants need to take a careful look at how their informal behavior may be interpreted. Thus, in these situations, more formal acknowledgment of meeting manners may be appropriate.

Remembering that everyone is important and truly being present in a meeting situation can be the basis for effective interpersonal communication in these situations.

KEY POINTS

1. Effective interpersonal communication is fundamental to the strategic achievement of a variety of managerial goals and is necessary for successful group and mass media encounters.

2. The current and past relationship you have with another person will have a significant effect on your ability to get your message across in interpersonal situations.

3. Every encounter you have with any individual, no matter how seemingly insignificant, will have a potential effect on the type of communication you can achieve when the need arises.

4. There are many myths about interpersonal communication and managers must rid themselves of such misconceptions.

5. Negative behaviors such as yelling, finger-pointing, stonewalling, or whining are not conducive to goal achievement in strategic communication.

6. It is important to understand other's viewpoints so that you can introduce an issue in a way that is important to them, ensuring that they will listen to, and try to understand, your message.

NOTES

1. Trenholm, S. and A. Jensen. 1988. *Interpersonal Communication.* Belmont, CA: Wadsworth.
2. Burleson, C. 1990. *Effective Meetings: The Complete Guide.* New York: John Wiley & Sons Inc., p. 116.

FOR YOUR BOOKSHELF . . .

Adler, Ronald and Jeanne Elmhorst. 1995. *Communicating at Work: Principles & Practices for Business and the Professions.* McGraw-Hill Ryerson.

Holtje, James. 1997. *Manager's Lifetime Guide to the Language of Power.* Prentice Hall.

Stewart, John. 1994. *Bridges Not Walls: A Book About Interpersonal Communication.* McGraw-Hill Ryerson.

Wilson, Gerald, and Michael Hanna. 1997. *Communicating in Business and Professional settings.* McGraw-Hill Ryerson.

ON THE WEB . . .

A Guide to Grammar & Writing
http://webster.commnet.edu/hp/pages/darling/grammar.htm

Purdue University On-Line Writing Lab
http://owl.english.purdue.edu

The Elements of Style
http://www.bartleby.com/141/index.html

Statistics Help for Writers
http://robertniles.com/stats

Acronym Finder

http://www.acronymfinder.com

University of Maryland Virtual Reference Room

http://www.inform.umd.edu/LibInfo/reference_room

Writing Effective E-Mail

http://www.delta.edu/~mmay/effective E-mail.html

(More) Writing Effective E-Mail

http://www.dbcc.cc.flus/fipse_sh/offectiveemail.htm

Put It in Writing

The difference between the right word and the almost right word is the difference between lightning and the lightning bug.

— Mark Twain

SURELY EVERY PERSON who makes his or her way into a managerial position in healthcare has adequate writing skills. Surely everyone who has graduated from college or university can write better than the average person. If you believe what William Zinsser says about writing (and you should), then you know that "Few people realize how badly they write."[1] And many healthcare managers are guilty of this.

But the fact remains: writing skills are critical to a manager's ability to communicate on a number of very important levels. In addition, *how* you write says more about you than you may have intended to say. In this case, with apologies to Marshall McLuhan, the writing in the medium is the message.

As you read this, take a mental journey through your own shelf of reference books. You should have the following:

- a good dictionary
- a medical dictionary
- a copy of *The Elements of Style*
- a copy of *The Elements of Grammar* (or a reasonable facsimile)
- a good book on business writing

If you lack even one of these books, you probably haven't given enough thought to the quality of your writing. And writing is something that a healthcare administrator does every day. What's more, evidence supports the notion that people who write well, think well. In other words, if you can organize your thoughts and select appropriate words to succeed in getting your message across to your audience accurately, you are probably a clear thinker. In fact, some managers even use this as a kind of litmus test when hiring new employees whose job responsibilities require them to be clear thinkers.

If we consider when and where a healthcare manager's writing skills are tested, we develop a kind of snapshot of the manager's job. Here are just a few of the situations where your own writing skills tell important tales about you as a communicator:

- e-mail
- memos
- letters
- reports and proposals
- minutes
- opinion pieces
- annual report letter
- editing employees' work
- clearing news releases
- articles for the employee or donor newsletter
- speeches and presentations

And the list goes on. Even if you have public relations personnel and administrative assistants to help you with these pieces, are you always so confident about the quality of *their* writing that you sign as if you had created it yourself? If you are at a lower level in the organizational hierarchy, you probably have to do your own writing, and the quality of your written communication will have a significant effect on your ability to climb to a higher level in that hierarchy.

Thus, it is clear that your own ability as a writer is a critical managerial skill. Let's examine how we determine what good writing is and then assess your own abilities in this area: how do *you* stack up?

WHAT THE HECK IS STYLE, ANYWAY?

The notion of considering your own writing style may bring back memories, good or bad, from high school and university English teachers. They always seemed to be talking about style, usually related to a particular writer: Ernest Hemingway, Mark Twain, Jane Austen, or William Shakespeare. And while you may have even developed a sense of the differences in the individual writers' styles, that seems years ago and miles away from a healthcare setting and the kind of writing that you are required to do as a manager. But is it really? That depends upon how you define style.

A dictionary is always a good place to start (especially when you are writing). Webster's defines style as the "manner of expressing thought, in writing or speaking: distinctive or characteristic form of expression."[2] This sounds very much like what your high school teacher was trying to impart to you as you studied English literature. It also has some information for us as we develop our skills in writing on the job. Style certainly is your manner of expressing thought in writing, but we need to add to this the notion of expressing thought for a particular audience and purpose. Unlike Hemingway and Twain, or your current favorite author, written communication in healthcare is done not simply to express the author's thoughts, but to achieve a specific purpose for a specific audience. (We will discuss this further later in the chapter.)

Another way of defining style, however, is a bit more pragmatic, and perhaps for our current purposes, even more useful. In 1919, English professor William Strunk wrote and self-published *The Elements of Style*, a book which has become like a bible to many writers. Years later one of his students, E.B. White, added his name to the author list and we have what is now reverently referred to simply as "Strunk and White," and often cited as the final word on style. Most of Strunk and White is devoted to considering style as "what is correct, or acceptable, in the use of English."[3] In other words, the correct use of grammar, syntax (word order), word choice, and punctuation are an important part of style. And the reality of writing in business and the professions is that correct writing says much more about you than simply whether you can make your point.

Have you ever received a letter (perhaps a cover letter for a job application) that was riddled with spelling and/or typographical errors? What was your first impression of that person? Are you even confident enough of your own grasp of style to be able to determine all the errors?

GOOD WRITING IS...

If you listen to the sound of your words—yes, read them aloud—you begin to get a sense of the style of your writing. Your style is your own unique way of expressing your thoughts. But this is not enough in work situations. Keep in mind that your own personal style isn't necessarily good writing. You can write whatever you want in your personal journal that no one else reads (and I highly recommend doing so), but your writing on the job must meet a litmus test of a different set of criteria. Here are some of those criteria by which you may judge the quality of your writing.

1. *Good writing is accurate.* Nothing can harm your credibility more quickly than when a reader finds that you have not been accurate. This is even more important in healthcare, where inaccuracies can have deleterious effects on people's health.

2. *Good writing is truthful.* Just as in everything else that you do, integrity is paramount. Truthfulness does not, however, necessarily mean telling everything. You need to be able to exercise judgment when you are disclosing sensitive information, or when you are approving the disclosure by others in your work group.

3. *Good writing is utilitarian.* When you are writing in business situations, it is important that what you write has a purpose. Just as you are too busy to read material that has no purpose for you, consider others—good writing is useful for you, the communicator, and for your reader. It is your challenge to ensure that what is useful for you is perceived to be useful by the receiver.

4. *Good writing is clear.* Vague, murky writing, choking on too many words, fails to achieve its goals. If you like to use big words in places where smaller ones will do, get over it. Be clear and concise at all times.

5. *Good writing is well-organized.* As we discussed earlier, well-organized writing often signifies a clear thinker. Looking at this another way, clear thinking must precede any writing and a good outline helps to organize.

6. *Good writing is complete.* There is no point in writing something if you are not prepared to provide all the required details to ensure an appropriate response. Make sure the reader has all the necessary information to understand your message.

7. *Good writing is targeted.* Every piece of writing you do must consider its audience. Knowing who will read your message is just as important as the message itself, and should guide you as you write.

One final piece of advice on good writing has stuck with me since I read it somewhere many years ago. I believe that the most important rule of good writing is never to bore your reader. While you might consider much of what you write to be mundane, day-to-day information exchange, you know that even an e-mail that fails to grab your attention in the first line or two gets only a skim from you, while an interestingly written one compels you to read it. Which scenario do you want played out on the receiving end of the e-mails that you take your own time to compose?

DIFFERENT STYLES, DIFFERENT PURPOSES

What was the purpose of that memo you just wrote to your managers? Why did you e-mail a response to that family who was looking for information about their mother's hospitalization? Was there a reason for you to write that opinion piece in the local paper after their scathing series on local healthcare facilities?

There are many reasons for using written communication and each instance has a unique purpose that you must consider before you write. The reason for the piece of writing has a huge effect on its style and on the outcome that you are likely to achieve. Both purpose and the resultant style, however, are also tied into the audience for the communication. We will discuss audience in detail shortly, but for now we will concentrate on answering the question "why" for each piece of writing.

STYLE

Three key components that differentiate one style from another are its pace, the tone that is taken, and sentence construction.[4]

While each individual writer can develop his or her own style of writing, there are essentially four styles that we tend to use in healthcare situations.

1. *Business style.* This is probably the most commonly used style, and even it has variations. Business style is characterized by directness, relative impersonality, and speed of coming to the point. Effective business writing is fast-paced, has a boardroom tone of voice, and uncomplicated sentence structure.

2. *Academic style.* You would have used academic style when you wrote research papers in college. In healthcare settings, you are more likely to read academic papers than to write them, but you need to be aware of this style so that you don't mistake it for business or any other style of writing. (Indeed, if you are interested, you may find yourself collaborating on academic papers as well.) Academic writing is characterized by complete impersonality, remoteness, objectivity, detailed attribution, and a scholarly tone. Its pace is slower and more ponderous than business writing (although one might reasonably question why this has to be so), takes on a very impersonal, third-person style, and can contain more complicated sentence constructions. It presumes that the reader is highly educated and very interested in the subject area.

3. *Feature style.* Feature writing is the style that is characteristic of magazine writing (or, in the healthcare manager's case, the employee newsletter). In a modified form, it will also be useful for the fundamentals of a presentation, and sometimes in proposals or for opinion/editorial pieces. It is characterized by a relatively rapid pace, a familiar tone, and uncomplicated sentence structure.

4. *Personal style.* In healthcare situations, this kind of writing is usually relegated to written communication with individuals with whom you are well-acquainted. It can vary in its

pacing, has a first-person personable tone, and relies on simple structures. In any business situation we need to be wary of too much familiarity and use this style judiciously. Extreme caution needs to be taken when creating e-mail correspondence, where this style can easily creep in.

It should be clear by now that each of these styles has a particular purpose and a specific target audience. You need to think very carefully about each piece you write *before* you write it—even when responding to what you consider to be routine correspondence.

PURPOSE

Written communication in the management of healthcare services and organizations has two main objectives. The first is a very simple, one-way approach: to provide information. The second is much more complicated than it appears on the surface: to induce someone to act.

1. *Providing information.* Arguably, providing information can be considered fundamental to any other objective one might have in communication. Indeed, it is difficult if not impossible to induce someone to take the action you desire if that person lacks clear, accurate, understandable information. This means that the better you are at providing information to a variety of different audiences, the better you will be at achieving your objectives.
2. *Inducing action.* The second objective for your written communication is to induce someone to take the action that you want or need that person to take. This involves perhaps even more planning and may require a number of steps.

Obviously, the first step is to provide the appropriate level of information, and at the same time to open a dialogue for two-way communication—feedback on the information received. This allows you to clarify and enhance. Then you move into finding the best way to get action.

PERSUASION

There are essentially only four ways to get other people to do what we want them to do:

1. payment
2. patronage
3. pressure
4. persuasion

Your written argument could contain elements of any or all of these, but essentially should be concerned with the last—persuasion—only.

First, you can, indeed, pay people to get them to do what you want them to do. In the case of management in healthcare, that usually means hiring. Enticing someone to do something by offering more money is a good approach under certain circumstances: if it is ethical, if you have no other option, and if you have the money. This is generally for only very specialized situations.

You could take the second approach and call in a favor. Patronage, in this sense, refers to convincing someone to do something for you because you have done something for them, or you might offer to do something in the future. This might work as the basis for your argument if you know your audience well and have a concrete, ethical foundation upon which to base this.

The third approach, pressure, could just as easily be termed coercion. It is highly suspect as an approach because it has long-term, negative ramifications for your relationship with the person or organization on the receiving end. If your written communication seems to have an undertone of threat to the receiver, you are failing to consider the implications of your action and you have not spent enough time considering how to develop the content of your written communication.

Although you may have been inclined to term each of the above *persuasion* techniques, in fact, from a communication perspective, they are not. You must consider changing how you think about persuasion. For our purposes, we can define persuasion as the use of communication strategies to change the way someone thinks about an issue—the pictures that person has in his or her head—so that he or she changes behavior in the direction that the communicator wants. This requires you to consider the images that might be elucidated by the words that you select in your written communication.

Three ways of thinking about the words you select are using positive images, using negative images, or using logic. If you paint a positive picture, you are inviting the receiver to move toward that image, to be a part of it. If you paint a negative image, then you are trying to make the receiver feel uncomfortable enough about it that he or she wishes to change behavior away from that image. Finally, you may have an unemotional issue that does not lend itself to either a particularly positive or negative image. This is when you take Aristotle's approach and create a logical argument. It is often particularly useful to use this as a supplement to the more emotional approaches for long-term effect. Research on emotionally laden persuasion approaches has found that the results are fast, but short-lived. Logic takes much longer to penetrate the mind of the receiver, but has more lasting effects.

The overriding objectives for all of your written communication should be to maintain and enhance a positive relationship with the receiver of the message.

WRITE FOR YOUR READER

Throughout this discussion about what to write, when, and for what reason, we have continually hearkened back to the reader, the receiver of your written communication. The notion of knowing as much as possible about your receiver holds true for any kind of communication, but can be forgotten in the daily grind of completing our written communication requirements.

You have a number of audiences with whom you will need to communicate in writing and each of them is different. They have different backgrounds, different levels of education, different types of relationships with you and your organization, and they have differing levels of interest in the topic about which you are writing. They also have different preferences for the medium used for receiving important information. Does your board request detailed reports? Do your colleagues favor letters? Do your employees prefer e-mails? Considering each of these factors is a key element in achieving your communication goals.

MYTHS ABOUT WRITTEN COMMUNICATION

We all have certain beliefs about writing and how we write. Holding on to false beliefs can impede our success. Here are some commonly held myths about writing.

1. *Good managers are good writers.* While this may, indeed, be true in some cases, one does not have any true relationship to the other. Many managers are particularly poor writers. In fact, there is no reason to believe that a manager will be any better at written communication than anyone at a lower level on the organizational hierarchy. Writing is a skill that must be consciously developed over time and the only way to become a good writer is to write.

2. *If you can write for one type of audience, you can write for anyone.* Wrong. If you can write well for one audience (college professors, perhaps?), bravo. But suggesting that this can be extrapolated to other audiences has no foundation. Each audience has different needs (as we have already discussed), and you will likely find that writing for some audiences is easier and more satisfying than writing for others.

3. *Everyone who graduates from college has a good grasp of style (grammar, syntax, punctuation, and word choice).* When was the last time someone discussed placement of commas, semi-colons, conjunctions, and the use of the subjunctive tense with you? For most college graduates, it has not been recently, unless you studied writing specifically. When was the last time you pulled out your style reference, or even your dictionary?

4. *Your reader is just as interested in your topic as you are.* This is almost never true, unless you are responding to something that originated with your reader, in which case it is more likely that *you* are less interested. Interest level is a very personal thing and something about which you should gather information, especially when you are trying to persuade someone. For example, if you are trying to convince your board about an issue, you need to begin by determining how everyone feels about the issue before developing a persuasive approach.

CLUTTER

No discussion of effective written communication would be complete without reference to what William Zinsser calls the "disease of American writing."[5] That, of course, is clutter, and no where else—with the possible exception of government documents—is cluttered writing more sprinkled with jargon and unnecessary words than in healthcare communication.

Consider the following memo from the manager of an outpatient department to her booking clerks:

In an effort to streamline the booking of appointments in the outpatient clinic, staff members are to be advised that the prioritization of patients will be completed prior to providing the patient with the appointment time. This will necessitate telephoning patients and advising them of their appointment times rather than being able to provide such appointment times during the initial telephone encounter.

Huh? Look at all the unnecessary words. The more unnecessary words, the greater the chance of misunderstanding. A less cluttered and clearer way to say this in a written memo or e-mail is:

When patients call to make appointments, they are to be ranked in order of priority and telephoned later with their appointment times.

DIFFERENT FORMATS, DIFFERENT RULES

There was a time when the memorandum was the backbone of business communication. Everyone now accepts that electronic transmission of what used to go into memos has made a huge difference in how we use the written word to communicate. However, many people have altered their writing for electronic transmission with little thought about good writing for this specific medium. Clearly, different formats require different rules.

E-MAIL

Electronic mail has been a godsend to many busy executives. The quick turnaround that it requires is a huge advantage for efficiency. However, this rapidity has also caused some writing problems to creep into such communication. While e-mail is generally accepted to be less formal than other types of written communication, this can, and often is, taken too far. Here are some things to keep in mind.

- The subject line is extremely important. Ensure that it is clear, descriptive, and to the point.
- The body should have a salutation. Don't simply launch in. If you know the recipient well, you might begin with a simple "hello." Otherwise, "Dear . . ." is suitable.
- Don't ramble on. Keep the message brief. Some people suggest keeping the message to about 25 lines, or one screen.[6] Anything longer should be sent as an attachment.
- Use short paragraphs and always proof the message before you send it! Typos are so common in e-mails, largely because many people who use e-mail are poor typists. Errors in e-mails provide the same subliminal messages as errors in other types of writing.

NEWS RELEASES

While you may not be the one actually writing the news release, as a manager you need to be aware of the rules of this special format.

- News releases should contain news and not be sent on a regular basis. They should only be released when there is a specific, actual news item to relate.
- The audience for the news release may ultimately be the general public, but its first audience is an editor or journalist. Therefore, it should be written in newspaper style.
- News releases use the "inverted pyramid" structure. The most important who, what, when, where, and why should be

in the first paragraph. The rest of the details can be filled in throughout the piece.

- News releases usually require a quote attributed to someone in the organization who is a credible source of information for the topic.

OPINION PIECES/EDITORIALS

As a healthcare manager it is very likely that you will be required to produce such a piece of writing at some point in your career. In fact, you should be looking for such opportunities. Here are some pointers about this format.

- Select the media outlet for your opinion piece carefully. Ensure that the readership of the particular newspaper is a large part of your intended target audience.
- Write professionally, but personably. Keep your points clear and simple. Avoid jargon, but if you must use it, explain it.
- Keep the piece to between 600 and 800 words.

NEWSLETTER PIECES

No matter what your level on the organizational hierarchy, you should consider the internal newsletter (print or electronic) to be an important venue through which employees can get to know you and you can provide important information. You should seek out opportunities to use this medium. Here are some pointers for healthcare managers and their contributions to internal newsletters.

- Ensure absolute accuracy! This is a rule for all forms, but you cannot afford even one slip-up with your internal audience. Your credibility and future relationships depend on trust.
- Use a crisp, clear style.[7] Avoid the use of adjectives and adverbs and stick to the subject and its action. People do not

spend a lot of time reading organizational newsletters, so get to the point. Keep it short and simple.

Each of these kinds of writing (as well as any others you may have to do) has specific issues that govern their successful accomplishment. In the final analysis, however, the important thing is to ensure that your writing is *readable*.

MAKING YOUR WRITING READABLE

If no one reads what you write there is little point in writing it. As a manager you write to accomplish a variety of goals, not, like the creative writer, for the love of it. You may be able to bring a subtle artistic flair to what you write, but you must consider a number of concrete approaches that ensure your writing will be read.

The first rule of readable writing is to simplify the complex. Knowing your audience helps you to do this without insulting the intelligence of your readers. If you are trying to explain an upcoming merger to your employees, go one step at a time. Most healthcare workers will have had little business experience and the process may seem complex and outside their realm.

Second, each individual element must be coherent. For example, as your teachers told you, the first (or topic) sentence of a paragraph indicates what that paragraph should be about. Writing that lacks this kind of coherence is difficult to follow and therefore not readable.

Third, select the correct word. Remember the Mark Twain quote at the beginning of this chapter? That says it all. C.S. Lewis added to this sentiment when he said, "Don't use words too big for the subject. Don't say 'infinitely' when you mean 'very,' otherwise you'll have no word left when you want to talk about something infinite."

Fourth, readable writing uses as little jargon as possible. Again, jargon use is related to the audience for your piece;

however, you probably should consider your audience and then use even less.

Finally, readable writing does not insult anyone. Avoid sexism, stereotyping, ageism, and all other subtleties that may have a negative effect on anyone. Re-read all your writing and purge it of these negative habits.

When you have completed a writing piece, make a point of reading it out loud. You will begin to hear the sound of your words and will be able to pick up problems more quickly than if you simply read it silently.

WRITING RESOURCES

Because writing is so fundamental to communication, I want to make specific mention of writing resources. Countless books and web sites are available to help you improve your writing. Listed at the end of the chapter are some of the more useful ones I have found, and several tests and crib sheets for your personal use.

KEY POINTS

1. Writing skills are critically important to a manager's ability to communicate.

2. *How* you write may say more about you than *what* you write.

3. In writing for healthcare management, style is your manner of expressing your thoughts to meet specific objectives for specific audiences.

4. The four styles of writing with which managers must be familiar are business, academic, feature, and personal.

5. One important goal of managerial writing is persuasion, which can be defined as using communication strategies to change the way someone else thinks about a topic or issue.

6. The overriding objective for all your writing should be to maintain and enhance a positive relationship with the receiver of the message.

NOTES

1. Zinsser, W. 1980. *On Writing Well.* New York: Harper & Row, Publishers, p. 19.
2. *New Illustrated Webster's Dictionary of the English Language.* 1992. New York: PMC Publishing Company, p. 957.
3. Strunk, W. and E. B. White. 1979. *The Elements of Style.* 3rd ed. New York: MacMillan Publishing Company, p. 66.
4. Alred, G., W. Oliu and C. Brusaw. 1992. *The Professional Writer.* New York: St. Martin's Press.
5. Zinsser, *op.cit.*, p. 7.
6. Http://www.delta.edu/ mmay/effectiveE-mail.html
7. Newsom, D. and B. Carrell. 1998. *Public Relations Writing: Form and Style.* 5th ed. Belmont, CA: Wadsworth Publishing Company.

CRIB SHEET 1:   CLUTTER

Don't use this . . .	Use this . . .
slowed down	slowed
in the near future	soon
at this point in time	now
at the present time	now
four o'clock in the afternoon	four p.m.
past history	history
very unique	unique
along the lines of	like
is in the process of planning	is planning
completely destroyed	destroyed
rose to the defence of	defended
be in need of	need
at all times	always
due to the fact that	because
give assistance to	help
in order to	to
make use of	use
make payment for	pay
on numerous occasions	often

CRIB SHEET 2:   EDITING PROBLEMS

The following are some words that the not-so-trusty spellchecker on your compter won't pick up when used in error:

accept	except
adapt	adopt
affect	effect
appraise	apprise
canvas	canvass
complement	compliment
dual	duel
further	farther
grisly	grizzly
naval	navel
parameter	perimeter
pore	pour
reign	rein/rain
stationary	stationery
their	there
then	than

TEST YOURSELF: HOW DOES YOUR WRITING STACK UP?

Section 1

Active voice is stronger and therefore almost always preferable to passive voice. Edit the following sentences to ensure that they're in active voice.

1. Control of the furnace is provided by the thermostat.

2. Fuel cost savings were realized through the installation of thermal insulation.

3. The policy manual is frequently updated by the supervisor's secretary.

4. Medical coverage in the emergency department will be provided by medical Emergency Specialists Inc.

Section 2

Purging clutter from your writing is essential to enhancing its readability. Rewrite the following sentences to get rid of the clutter.

1. It is most useful to keep in mind that the term Alzheimer's Disease refers to a whole spectrum of symptomatology.

2. It is unfortunate that I was unavailable to you when you visited out hospital facility on Monday.

3. It has come to the attention of management that there has been excessive smoking carried out by various employees close to the front doors, and thus we have come to the decision that there is to be a new policy that smoking within fifty feet of any doorway is to be stopped immediately and for the future.

FOR YOUR BOOKSHELF . . .

Moreno, Mary. 1997. *The Writer's Guide to Corporate Communications.* Allworth Press.

Shertzer, Margaret. 1986. *The Elements of Grammar.* Collier Books.

Strunk, William and E. B. White. 2000. *The Elements of Style,* 4th ed. Allyn & Bacon.

Zinsser, William. *On Writing Well.* 1998. Harper and Row.

5

Presentations That Deliver

The ability to speak is a short cut to distinction. It puts
a man in the limelight, raises him head and shoulders
above the crowd, and the man who can speak accept-
ably is usually given credit for an ability out of all proportion to what he really possesses.

— Lowell Thomas

IT IS OFTEN said that speaking in public is ranked as the
number-one fear of the average North American, outdistancing
even the fear of spiders and snakes.[1] But if you are a healthcare
executive, speaking in public is not an option—it is an absolute
requirement. Whether you are giving a presentation to an employee group, your board, a government agency, a community
group, or your peers, speaking well can not only help you to
achieve specific objectives for your organization, but it can also
contribute to the development of your own career as a healthcare
executive. Times have changed for speakers and audiences.

Bert Decker, author of *You've Got to Be Believed to Be Heard*[2]
suggests that the Winston Churchills of the world have given
way to the Norman Schwarzkopfs—those who can command
more than $60,000 for each speaking engagement because they
are able to engage the audience's emotions. Roger Ailes writes

in his speaking primer *You Are the Message* that one of the most common problems in communication is "presentation of material that is intellectually oriented, forgetting to involve the audience emotionally."[3] This means that the way you may have learned to deliver speeches (Never do this! Making speeches and delivering presentations are two different things. Stick to making presentations.) may be outdated and ineffective with the audiences you will face today. Today's audiences, whether employee groups or the chamber of commerce, are children of the television age, a fact that has changed the way they view entertainment, information, persuasion, and source credibility.

Let's examine the why and how of making effective presentations that will enhance both your job and your career in healthcare today. Then we will examine how you stack up.

MAKING YOUR PRESENTATIONS STRATEGIC

Anyone working at any level of healthcare management must be able to make presentations. For some healthcare executives, making a presentation in public is as natural as brushing their teeth. For others, it is like a non-swimmer contemplating jumping off the back of a cruise ship—a terrifying experience that can and should be avoided. Between these two extremes is the majority that believes it is a necessary evil. But even mandatory presentations have a strategic component to them.

If we examine just the minimal qualifications necessary as a manager of any kind, it becomes clear that, even at this level, making presentations is a requirement. For example, it is now well established that front-line employees want to receive important information face-to-face[4] (more about that in Chapter 6) rather than in written memos, newsletters, or e-mails. This means that as a manager you are required to present informative and often persuasive messages to employee groups on a fairly regular basis. While these groups may be small for managers at lower levels on the hierarchy, as your career in health administration progresses, the size of these employee groups will grow as well.

Other areas within your role as a healthcare manager where presentation skills are increasingly important are in dealing with boards and government agencies. Often the healthcare manager is in the position of attempting to lobby or otherwise pitch something to these groups. Finely honed presentation skills are an important factor in the success of these efforts.

There may be some times when presentation skills may seem at first glance to be completely optional. However, for a career-minded professional, these seemingly voluntary situations are not. Whether you like it or not, as an administrator in healthcare, you are often viewed by the general public as a kind of expert in healthcare. While community groups may be inclined to see a doctor (or in some cases a nurse) as a *health* expert, you are a *healthcare* expert—and if your community doesn't see you that way yet, you need to take steps to place yourself in that position. This means that you may indeed have a responsibility to help others to understand the healthcare system, and as such will need to make yourself available to address interested community groups. This is increasingly crucial today as healthcare consumers are acutely concerned about the future of their healthcare delivery systems.

This has a two-fold result from your perspective. It not only provides much-needed accurate information for the general public, which can help your organization with its important messages, but it also serves to enhance your own profile in the community. This is beneficial both for the public image of your organization in meeting its community responsibilities as well as for your own image.

Other instances in which you may find yourself needing highly developed presentation skills include opportunities for you to bring your experience and expertise to your peers. Participating in workshops, seminars, and conferences for health professionals, trustees, and other healthcare managers provides you with an opportunity to give something to your profession, as well as to enhance your own professional profile in the healthcare community. Have you ever passed up these opportunities because you do not feel as comfortable as you would like to in making presentations? This is very common.

In this same vein, you may also have the opportunity to bring that experience and expertise to students in healthcare and healthcare management. Your skills as a presenter will allow you to respond positively the next time an instructor or professor calls seeking a guest lecturer.

Whether making presentations is required or optional, you still need to exercise some strategic thinking in selecting when and where to make those presentations. This decision derives directly from the objectives you have in making that presentation. For employee groups, you may be able to control not only the venue of the presentation but the size of the group as well. If you are bringing bad news, such as lay-off information, you may find it useful to make the groups small and the opportunities for immediate feedback greater.

If you wish to make presentations to community groups, should you say yes to every request? Probably not. Should you seek out your own opportunities? Definitely, yes. In general, the presentations you make need to fit in with the overall objectives that your hospital or healthcare agency has for its relationship with the community (more about this in Chapter 9).

In strategically selecting venues for public speaking, you should take a proactive approach. Don't always wait for situations in which you will be on the responding end. Consider the overall goals of your organization on an annual basis and make plans to use your presentation skills to achieve specific objectives. Then, when you find yourself in a reactive situation, the audience that you face (the board or employees, perhaps), will already be familiar and positively disposed to your presentation style.

PREPARATION

The first rule of making presentations is to be fully prepared. This is one of the most effective ways to deal with stage fright. Even if you see yourself as a seasoned and comfortable speaker, never neglect this step. And while preparation involves more than making an outline of the topic to be covered, it is a good place to start.

AUDIENCE

As you sit down at your desk and consider what to say, begin by describing for yourself, in as detailed a fashion as possible, the audience you will face. The following questions may help you to tailor your presentation to this group.

1. *How does this group relate to you in terms of organizational hierarchy?* This is always applicable when you are presenting to internal groups, and may be useful for some external groups.
2. *How familiar are they with this subject?* The more familiar they are, the more appropriate it is for you to use related jargon; otherwise, avoid it entirely. You may also not need so much background if they already know it. Give your audience some credit.
3. *How interested are they in this subject?* An audience that fails to share your enthusiasm for a topic area will especially need to be drawn into it emotionally, or they will tune out.
4. *How large is the group?* The size of the group often dictates the degree of formality, the level of audience interaction you will be able to achieve, and the visuals you will need to prepare.

The answers to these questions will help you to determine a variety of factors including approach, language, tone, visuals, and, believe it or not, even what you should wear.

OPENINGS

Once you are familiar with whom you will be presenting to and with your objectives for making the presentation, you are ready to begin preparing an outline. The place to begin is at the beginning. How will you start your presentation?

There are several approaches you can consider. Some people believe a joke is a terrific opener for a presentation. As a health-care manager, however, exercise extreme caution in using this kind of an opening. It might be a good way to start if: (a) you know your audience well, such as your employee group; (b) the topic is a positive one (it may not be a good idea to begin with a joke just as you are about to inform them of lay-offs); (c) the joke is carefully selected; and (d) you are capable of delivering a joke well (and this is not a universal skill). If all of these criteria are met, go ahead. Otherwise, you should select another way to break the ice.

Feature writers in magazines have a few ways that they usually start an article. These openings are just as useful in making presentations.

1. *Anecdote*. One of the most effective ways to begin to draw an audience emotionally into your presentation is to tell a story. The story should illustrate a human side of the topic and should be one with which this particular audience may be able to identify on some level. It can be a humorous story (which differs from a joke) if the topic is a light-hearted one. More often, when we are talking about healthcare issues, the anecdote is a more emotional one. It might even be a personal story, if it suits the topic, and can be a very good approach when speaking to your peers. The story itself should not be too long, but needs a beginning, middle, and an end. Occasionally, you might save the end of the story until the close of your presentation.

2. *Startling fact.* This could be a statistic that is not likely to be known already by your audience, something that happened, a startling amount of money, something that is quick, to the point, and wakes up your audience. It can be very effective if selected well.

3. *Quotation.* Some speakers place the well-selected quote on a slide and let the audience read it while they are preparing to listen. This allows them a minute or two to absorb it before you begin talking about it. (This same approach can also be used when you use a *question* to begin your presentation.)

Whatever approach you choose to begin your presentation, you need to plan it in advance. Then provide the audience with a brief outline of what you intend to talk about on this occasion. Be specific about the purpose of the presentation and where you will end up at the end.

Occasionally it can be useful to tell the audience something more about yourself than may have been conveyed during your introduction (if you have been introduced). This is obviously unnecessary in internal presentations that are centered on day-to-day activities of your organization. If your audience is at all likely to ask the question "What the heck is this person doing here talking to us about this?" then you may need to present yourself and your credentials briefly. Ensure that this is not perceived as patting yourself on the back. It should not be self-congratulatory in any way, only informative, addressing any anticipated concerns of your audience.

ORGANIZATION

The remainder of your outline should be the main points supported by the facts, information, and stories that augment each of them. There are various approaches to organizing material. The topic, objectives, and how you think about the subject will all play a role in which method you choose. Here are some of the methods:[5]

- *Topical.* Divide your subject into its component parts.
- *Chronological.* Topics that have a history or any kind of future timeline lend themselves to this approach.
- *Spatial.* You can map ideas using a visual aid.
- *Journalistic.* Organize the topic according to the who, what, when, where, why, and how.
- *Problem/Solution.* Select a problem for discussion and propose a solution.
- *Process of Elimination.* Eliminate alternatives and argue for the remaining option (especially effective when your presentation has a persuasive objective).
- *Motivational.* Use the psychological steps of gaining the audience's attention, establishing a need, satisfying the need, visualizing the results, and then providing some guidance for moving the audience to action.
- *Classical Judicial.* This is the provision of argument and counter argument and again can be useful when persuasion is your goal.

Because a presentation needs a beginning, a middle, and an end, you need to outline your wrap up. Provide a brief summary and then consider how you will actually end. If you haven't finished your beginning anecdote, then you have a ready-made ending. Otherwise, you may want to save a relevant quotation, a thought, or a call to action, if that is part of your objectives.

APPEARANCE

Before we move on to considering your approach to the subject, it might be a good time to consider what you will wear. While this may seem at first glance to be a frivolous matter for a serious healthcare manager, it is not. Today's audiences were brought up watching television and are fairly sophisticated about drawing conclusions based on visual presentation. Most communications experts believe, and have evidence to support, the fact that most of us make up our minds about someone on first impression in about seven seconds.[6] This means that how you look and the eye contact that you make will be either positive or negative input for the receiver of your message.

Deciding what to wear when making a presentation is actually just a marker for deciding how you will look to the audience in general, including the expression on your face and how much eye contact you make. Image consultant Catherine Graham Bell cites a great deal of research that concludes that, at least in job interview situations, personal presentation is the key factor in the decision about who will get the job and who will progress up the career ladder.[7] The same situation holds true when meeting people who are a part of your audience. They will make decisions about you before you even open your mouth. These first impressions can either help or hinder your ability to get your message across effectively. So, how will you present yourself?

As a healthcare manager, you represent a number of different constituencies besides yourself. Unlike the job interview where you represent only yourself, when making a public presentation you represent anything that the audience associates with you. This means that you are an ambassador for your healthcare organization, as well as the field of healthcare administration. Regardless of the venue or the audience you need to be perceived as a professional.

A good rule of thumb is to present yourself at one notch of formality up from that which you expect of your audience. If your audience will be wearing uniforms, you need to wear whatever you consider to be your best uniform. If you normally wear a uniform, too, this is what you should wear when making a presentation. But your uniform should be impeccable, even if theirs are not.

If you are presenting to an external group or your board, you need to be just one notch up. If you know that the group is quite casual, you cannot be quite as casual as they are. Even if you choose to dress casually, you need to look well-kept and professional.

YOUR APPROACH

How will you approach your topic? What kind of a tone will you employ? Aristotle believed that there are three ways that we can persuade others to our point of view: ethos, logos, and pathos. These three approaches are useful in determining your tone and style even if your prime objective is to provide information rather than to persuade.

The first approach you might take is to simply rest on your laurels, but I do not recommend it. Aristotle called this *ethos* and indicated that the audience's acceptance of the speaker's message was dependent in this case on the believability of the speaker. Although this can't be the total basis of your approach, it may be a useful guideline in helping you to determine how much of your own personal experience can be used. If you are perceived by this group to be credible, you can capitalize upon this and use your own perspective as a basic approach. On the other hand, if you lack credibility in their eyes, you need to include something that will help to build that believability.

Aristotle's second approach, *logos*, rests on the strength of facts and statistics, all of which are used to put together a logical argument to make a point. Logic has a positive effect in the long term, but often fails to engage your listener in the short term. Thus, if a lot of facts and figures are needed to make your points, it might also be useful to consider a more emotional approach — what Aristotle called *pathos*.

Because communication technology is sophisticated and audiences are almost as sophisticated, the use of an emotional approach can be very effective. As we discussed at the beginning of this chapter, the reason Schwarzkopf is in demand as a speaker is not because of his ability to expound political rhetoric, or even to list facts and figures, but because he is able to engage the emotions of his listeners. In healthcare, the potential for emotional connection is even greater than in many other areas. Indeed, health professionals need to guard against the very real possibility of exploiting this emotional hunger in audiences.

Each of these approaches on their own has limitations. Thus, in determining the approach you will take to a topic, you should consider including each of them in greater or lesser amounts. Your audience, objectives, and topic will dictate this.

SHOW AND TELL

We take in messages through all of our five senses. In fact, some studies have shown that the relative effect of the five senses in the learning process is 11 percent through hearing, 14 percent through taste, touch, and smell, and a whopping 75 percent through sight.[8] Australian speaking coach Doug Malouf says that a speaker is likely to achieve only 33 percent of his or her goals without visuals, but 67 percent with visuals[9]—a very compelling argument for always using visuals.

The reality is that you may not always be able to use visuals. It may be impossible or at least impractical to use visual aids when your presentation is very short, when you have been asked to speak in an impromptu situation (more about these situations later), or when the group is very small and intimate.

In general, your use of visual aids should increase proportionally with the size of the audience and the length of your presentation. A two-hour presentation to a conference of healthcare executives should make extensive use of visual aids, while a half-hour presentation to your board would include only a small number. Clearly, visuals are very important for your audience, but they are also important for you as the speaker. Well-designed slides or overhead transparencies not only reinforce what you are saying, but they provide you with a very clear outline for where to go next. Since you should *never memorize or deliver a speech*, they will guide you from point to point with very little shuffling of notes. There is nothing more impressive to an audience than a speaker who seems to need no notes — this goes a long way to enhance the speaker's credibility. In addition, shuffling through notes is often distracting for the audience. Use your visuals well.

Let's turn our attention to the practicalities of visuals — how to select them, prepare them, and use them.

SELECTION

In selecting the format and tone of the visuals, you need to think about the same audience considerations that you used in the preparation of your outline: size, type, interest, and knowledge levels. While you might use light-hearted visuals for a casual topic with a peer group, a serious topic may require a more polished look. The format you choose will depend on functional considerations such as the room size, availability, and portability. There is no point in selecting a slide presentation in a room so small that the slides will look like your vacation pictures hung on the wall. If you are going far afield, you must be able to transport your visuals, so a flip chart might not be a good idea. If you are speaking to a community group, check to make sure they have access to an overhead projector before you begin to prepare transparencies.

PRESENTATION

How many times have you gone to a conference and been faced with a presenter whose visuals were impossible to see from the back or so full of text that you couldn't even begin to read them? I have even passed classrooms where professors are using photocopied pages from books as transparencies. Unfortunately, these situations happen more often than they should.

There is nothing more effective than a well-thought-out, well-designed visual. Here are my very basic design considerations when preparing visuals to accompany a presentation:

- select a format and color scheme and keep it consistent
- keep them simple and uncluttered
- keep the background clear
- ensure that the type is a significant contrast to the background
- avoid large text blocks at all costs
- use large enough type
- avoid overly ornate type faces
- use lines and clip art sparingly
- use graphs, flow charts, and photos when appropriate

Should you use overhead transparencies, 35mm slides, a flip chart, or presentation software? Each of these has to be considered carefully.

An abundance of software is available today for developing visuals for presentation. It is, however, only as useful as the user's grasp of basic design. While many programs provide templates, not all are effective in all situations. I don't know about you, but I am sick of poorly developed computer presentations. If you do not know how to develop and use slides well, these computer-enhanced visuals are not going to save you. If you are going to use this method or one similar to it, consider the following.

1. The less contrast there is between the type and the background, the darker the room has to be (and darkened rooms are more conducive to sleeping than to taking notes).
2. Too many swirl-ins and rotate-outs can leave the audience feeling dizzy.
3. The darkness allows much less eye contact with your audience.

Sometimes the now seemingly old-fashioned overhead projector can be like a gift to both a speaker and an audience. With desktop publishing software and color printers so readily available, using the overhead can be as professional as some people perceive the use of the computer. The advantage of the overhead is that the room can remain light (with lights just over the screen off), and you can face your audience while still seeing what is on the screen.

One of the most common pitfalls in using the overhead is not knowing what it was designed to do. The overhead projector was designed to project over the speaker's head so that the speaker can maintain eye contact with the audience at all times. This means that turning around to read off the screen is not only inappropriate, it is unnecessary. When you need to point something out on the screen, you can do it with a pen on the projector surface, all the while maintaining eye contact. This avoids having your entire body silhouetted on the screen and being blinded upon your return while you attempt to point something out.

One final note about using visuals such as these: always manipulate your own slides and transparencies. If you are using an overhead projector, ensure that it is on the podium with you where you can reach it easily. If you are using a slide projector, use a remote. A remote can also be used for a notebook computer if it is not close enough for you to press a key. This avoids the need for continually interrupting your remarks with "Next slide, please!"

NEVER MAKE A SPEECH!

Whenever I hear that someone is going to "make a speech" I immediately start to yawn. While a well-delivered presentation can be life changing, unless you are a Martin Luther King Jr., you should avoid making speeches at all costs.

This may be a simple matter of semantics, but here is what I mean by a speech. Webster's defines a speech as "a public address; a discourse,"[10] and gives "a sermon"[11] as one of the definitions of a discourse. Need we say more?

One of the problems with speechmaking is that there is the tendency to read from a prepared text. When you are making a presentation, you should (a) never write out your entire presentation word for word, or (b) read. This also means that you should never get your public relations staff to write a speech for you. In fact, as speaking coach Don Aslett points out, "Professional speech writing is sad evidence that you really don't have anything to say . . . a message can't be very important if it isn't important enough for you to prepare it personally."[12]

IMPROMPTU SPEAKING

For every professional there comes a time when someone unexpectedly says, "Could you just say a few words?" Then it is up to you to think on your feet and say something coherent and useful. The key to these unexpected situations is to never let them be truly unexpected.

It is usually possible to anticipate situations where it is likely that someone might make such a request: at a board meeting, at the annual dinner honoring your long-time staff, or at a public meeting considering your hospital's application for expansion. Consider those Hollywood stars who aren't sure they will win the Oscar, but they always prepare their acceptance speech. Don't ever let yourself be completely unprepared.

The best motto you could adopt for these and most other communication situations is to *think before you speak*. As you rise to move toward the microphone, do so slowly and deliberately, thinking all the time. If you follow the second rule—*keep it short*—this brief moment of preparation will be enough to carry you through. As some people begin to talk, however, they start to prattle. Listen to yourself and try to connect with your audience to avoid this.

Finally, one of the best ways to ensure that your remarks are coherent and have a beginning, middle, and end is to *tell a story* if you can think of one quickly. It will always be better organized than a series of disconnected remarks.

COLLABORATION: THE TEAM APPROACH

Often, a team approach to a presentation can be a most effective tool for meeting your objectives. If a variety of expertise is required, you might consider a group of specialists. For example, if you are making a pitch for money to enlarge your emergency department you might consider asking both a physician and a nurse to present with you. If you are lobbying to change admission policies to your long-term care facility, you, your director of admissions, and even a family member might be a dynamic team. There are, however, some issues to consider when working as a team.

First, while each of you has a particular area of expertise, you need to organize the presentation as a whole. This means getting together to plan the objectives, approach, and tone. You also need to take an inventory of what each participant knows about the issue and the individual relationships with the proposed

audience. This overall organization also extends to your visuals —
they must be consistent. Once the planning is out of the way,
the group should rehearse together and determine how you will
handle the actual presentation.

There are two problematic aspects of speaking as a group.
The first is the way transitions are handled. There should be a
smooth lead-in to the next speaker by the previous one and you
need to consider carefully how the audience is likely to react to
bouncing back and forth from speaker to speaker. It can be very
distracting. In general, you should avoid organizing the material
so that it is necessary for any one person to speak more than once,
with the exception of the person who might open and close the
presentation.

The second concern is what to do while the others are speaking. The audience will see all of you and if one of you looks bored
or uninterested in what the others are saying, the audience will
pick this up. When you are not speaking, you should pretend you
are on camera at all times, because anything you do can and will
be picked up. Maintain your interest by unobtrusively nodding
and making the occasional note. And never interrupt or correct
the speaker!

Finally, you need to decide early on how you will handle
questions. It is most appropriate for each speaker to handle
questions, rather than having one do all the talking.

HOW DO YOU STACK UP?

Here are some questions that you might ask yourself to determine
just how well prepared you are for making presentations.

- When asked to speak, do you always ask the following
  questions:
  - How many people will be attending?
  - Who will the audience consist of?

- What do they know about this issue?
- Whose idea was it to present about this topic?
- How large is the room?
- How is the room laid out?
- What kind of audiovisual equipment is available?
- How long will I be speaking?
- Will others be speaking?
- If yes, what will they be speaking about and when will my presentation be in relationship to the others?

- Do you always spend some time thinking about how you will begin?
- Do you always prepare an outline?
- Do you always figure out what your objectives will be for the presentation (both for you and for your organization)?
- Do you always do more research than you think you will need?
- Do you always consider carefully the kind of visual impression that you will make on this particular audience?
- Do you prepare eye-catching, uncluttered visuals to support your presentation?
- Do you feel comfortable in the use of a variety of audiovisual approaches (overhead transparencies, 35mm slides, computer-based visuals, and flip charts)?
- Do you always speak approximately within the time that was allotted to you?
- Do you always avoid prattling on?
- Do you feel comfortable fielding questions?
- Do you ask to see any written evaluation that may be done by participants (e.g., at a conference)?

If you can honestly answer 'yes' to all of the above questions, then you stack up well against your peers. If, however, there are areas that you have failed to consider or where you feel uncomfortable, you may need to think about your presentations a bit more or even ask for outside coaching.

You cannot avoid making presentations in your career as a healthcare manager. Indeed, it is to both your advantage and that of your organization for you to seek out opportunities to put yourself in front of an audience to meet strategic organizational objectives.

KEY POINTS

1. Anyone in healthcare management must be able to make presentations to meet strategic objectives.

2. Today's most successful speakers are those who can engage their audiences rather than simply produce a list of facts and figures.

3. The first rule of making presentations that deliver is to be fully prepared in advance for both your topic and the specific audience.

4. Always prepare an outline. Never write out the full text (you might be inclined to read it).

5. Visual aids greatly enhance the potential that you will meet your goals for any presentation.

6. Good visuals are consistent, appropriate for both the topic and the audience, and are used knowledgeably during a presentation.

7. Even when asked to speak extemporaneously, think before you speak, outlining in your head what you will say, and then keep it short.

8. To meet certain strategic objectives, it is sometimes most effective to use a team approach to presentation.

Keep the title slide simple and clear. This format could be in color for slides or computer display, or overhead display. This landscape layout can be changed to portrait layout for overhead projection.

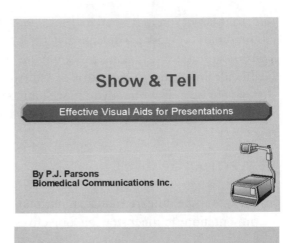

Provide a presentation outline in bullet format.

Use of a chart can enhance the visual impact of a statistic.

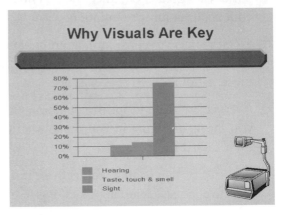

Choosing a Medium

- Composition of your audience
- Audience size
- Venue considerations

Ensure that your lines are short and that there are not too many.

Basic Design Considerations

- Consistency
- Simplicity
- Contrast
- Line limit
- Type face
- Artwork

It should be clear by now that you don't place your entire presentation on your visuals.

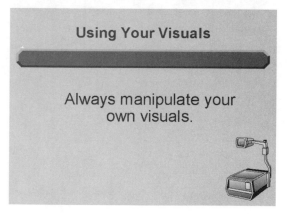

Using Your Visuals

Always manipulate your own visuals.

NOTES

1. Wallechinsky, D., I. Wallace, and A. Wallace. 1977. *The Book of Lists*. New York: Bantam Books, p. 469.
2. Decker, B. 1992. *You've Got to Be Believed to Be Heard*. New York: St. Martin's Press.
3. Ailes, R. 1988. *You Are the Message: Secrets of the Master Communicators*. Homewood, Illinois: Dow Jones-Irwin, p. 9.
4. Larkin, T. and S. Larkin. 1995. "Internal Communication: Have We Missed the Mark?" *IABC Communication World*, March, p. 13.
5. Http://www.abacon.com/pubspeak/organize/patterns.html
6. Ailes, *op cit.*
7. Bell, C. G. 1997. *Managing Your Image Potential*. Kingston, Ontario: Prime Impressions.
8. Malouf, D. 1988. *How to Create and Deliver a Dynamic Presentation*. Brookvale, NSW: Simon and Schuster Australia.
9. Malouf, *op cit.*
10. *New Illustrated Webster's Dictionary of the English Language*. 1992. New York: PMC Publishing Company, Inc., p. 926.
11. Webster's, p. 280.
12. Aslett, D. 1989. *Is There a Speech Inside You?* Cincinnati: Writer's Digest Books, p. 25.

FOR YOUR BOOKSHELF . . .

Aslett, Don. 1989. *Is There a Speech Inside You?* Writer's Digest Books.

Tierney, Elizabeth. 1996. *How to Make Effective Presentations.* Sage Publications.

Whalen, D. Joel. 1996. *I See What You Mean: Persuasive Business Communication.* Sage Publications.

ON THE WEB . . .

Allyn & Bacon's Public Speaking Web Site
http://www.abacon.com/pubspeak

How to Conquer Public Speaking Fear
http://www.stresscure.com/jobstress/speak.html

How to Give a Bad Talk
http://www.cs.wisc.edu/~markhill/conferencetalk.html#badtalk

University of Kansas—Virtual Presentation Assistant
http://www..ukans.edu/cwis/units/coms2/vpa/vpa.htm

LEVEL II

It All Begins at Home

Once you have taken into consideration why communication is important for a healthcare manager and have examined and enhanced your own skills for the job, you have set the stage for looking beyond yourself to the specifics of the audiences with whom you are required to communicate.

On the second level, we will examine the audiences closest to home. You will find some interesting peculiarities about such audiences as employees, medical staff, and boards of trustees. Each of these groups and others like them have a vested interest in the successful achievement of your organization's overall mission and operational goals, just as you do.

Crucial to your knowledge of and skills in communication is the extent to which you understand the public relations function of your organization. Even if your organization is a small one without a designated PR department, you still need to be concerned about the public relations aspects of your actions.

6
Communicating In-House

Start with good people, lay out the rules, communicate
with your employees, motivate them and reward them.
If you do all these things effectively, you can't miss.

— Lee Iacocca

NO MATTER HOW hard you might try, you can't avoid them.
They are your employees, your organization's volunteers, your
board members. They are the groups of people who are closest
to home, and like you have a vested interest in your organization.
How you communicate with them is key to achieving the goals
you have set.

At the beginning of the 1990s, the International Association
of Business Communicators, headquartered in San Francisco,
published the results of its study on the topic of organizational
communication with employees. Their results pointed directly
to the crucial importance of communication skills of managers
at all levels. They found that most employees want important
information to come directly to them, face-to-face from their
front-line managers; that these supervisory people are not communicating satisfactorily; that senior managers are all but invis-
ible to most employees; and that managers are not listening to

97

their employees.[1] This speaks poorly of the communication skills of today's managers, but more poorly about the importance managers place on communication close to home. In this chapter, we will examine this attitude toward communication, as well as the communication practicalities you face on a daily basis.

CHARITY (AND OTHER THINGS) BEGINS AT HOME

Consider the following scenario. Your hospital has been grappling with a budget deficit for the past two years. The employees are all aware of this and the uncertainty about the future has already resulted in a considerable slide in morale, with all of its concomitant problems. As employees drive to work for the morning shift, a radio news report leaks information about possible layoffs at your institution today. The employees arrive at work to face the possibility of termination and the 50 who actually receive pink slips are soon gone. Where does this leave the rest of your employees? More to the point, where does that leave you as a manager? How is your credibility? How do employees rate you in terms of your opinion of *their* importance? How important are employees?

Employees, medical staff, volunteers, and your board are crucial to your ability to accomplish anything at all. They are also your most important ambassadors to the outside world. So, not only is how you communicate with them important internally, but it also has a significant spin-off effect on the way you and your organization are perceived publicly.

Let's begin by examining your relationship (the outcome of your communication) with important internal groups. Consider your responses to the following questions.

- Do you generally feel comfortable when entering a meeting with each of the following groups?

- your peers   - medical staff
- your employees   - other health professionals
- patients   - your bosses

- Do you feel that the members of the above groups trust you? (What evidence do you have for your response?)
- Do you trust the members of the above groups?

The extent to which you have been able to nurture a positive relationship with each of these groups will affect your ability to achieve goals. How you communicate with them and why you do so are the key factors in these relationships.

THE HEALTHCARE CULTURE

Business schools like to talk a lot about *corporate culture*. Indeed, most healthcare managers who have formal education in administration will have studied the concept. Business schools, however, are notorious for neglecting to discuss in detail one of the most important contributing factors to the culture of the organization: communication. Both the general communication *climate* of the organization and the communication *style* of the senior managers are keys to deciphering the personality of the organization. If we are going to place internal communication into context, this is the best place to start.

CORPORATE CULTURE

We will begin by refreshing your memory about the concept of corporate culture. For many years, anthropologists were the only ones who seemed to be studying culture, defined in Webster's as "the sum total of the attainments and activities of any specific period, race or people, including their implements, handicrafts, agriculture, economics, music, art, religious beliefs, traditions, language and story."[2] So, we might use this as a template for defining organizational culture if we think of it as the history, mythology, beliefs, values, rituals, and jargon of any specific organization as they have evolved over time. By understanding an organization's cultural components, it is possible to begin to understand why the relationships exist as they are beyond any sense of logic. Relationships within organizations often defy logic. But why is it important to examine these relationships?

An organization's culture has often been referred to as the glue that holds it together. Strong cultures are characterized by high employee morale, a sense of shared vision, and high productivity. In healthcare that translates into high-quality services delivered by highly competent, satisfied, loyal employees.

MISSION AND VALUES

Many specific definitions of corporate culture exist: indeed, every writer seems to have developed his or her own definition. But several commonalities in the literature about corporate culture appear when we begin to examine the factors that serve to either enhance or detract from the strength of the culture. Obviously, a strong mission and core value system are important. We have already examined mission statements, but if you go back to the mission statement of your own organization, it is not enough that it sounds good and is well articulated. What is important here is how many of your employees actually know what the mission of your organization is, can relate it to others outside your organization, and actually buy into the values and philosophy.

One of the most striking examples of the strength a company gains from a shared value system was seen in the early 1980s when Johnson and Johnson faced what is now referred to by communication professionals as the "Tylenol Crisis." The company pulled their products off the shelves at an estimated cost to them of some $75 million, a major gamble in anyone's mind.

But how they came to the decision to do this is a striking example of a working philosophy doing its work.

Johnson and Johnson has a credo written in 1943 by the son of the company's founder. It starts off this way: "We believe our first responsibility is to the doctors, nurses, and patients, to mothers and all others who use our products and services." The extent to which this philosophy has been internalized into the company's decision-making process is reflected in the words of Robert Kniffen, senior vice-president of corporate relations, who was in the president's office at the time of the decision. He was quoted as saying: "It was not an instance where someone said, 'Let's consult the Credo and think through this problem,' but rather it was a way of looking at the world, at business and at a decision. The Credo structures the way you look at things."[3] A value system that is truly understood and embraced by an organization's employees is a powerful contribution to a strong culture—but it is not the only one.

HISTORY AND MYTHOLOGY

Another important factor in the development of a strong culture is a shared history and mythology. The history consists of the factual details of the organization's evolution, while the mythology develops from the stories that grow from that history.

Hospitals are especially fertile breeding grounds for mythology: the surgeon who throws instruments in the O.R. (no one has actually seen it happen, but everyone has heard about it), or the patient who was found dead in the laundry cart (no one knows when it happened, but everyone knows about it). Each of these shared stories helps to glue the employees together.

COMMUNICATION

One of the most important aspects of what makes a culture strong is directly related to you, the manager. The communication style of the managers, and the communication climate developed as a result, are keys to defining the organization's culture and, ultimately, the strength of the internal relationships.

A managerial communication style that fosters open, two-way communication within and among internal groups will have a significantly positive effect on the organizational climate. Employees and others who feel comfortable in both lauding as well as criticizing, and who recognize that someone will actually listen, are likely to have a stronger sense of loyalty, with a resultant increase in morale. Both the manager's verbal (oral and written) and non-verbal communication style will have an effect on the communication climate. It is also important to recognize that you may not be the best judge of your style.

Every year as I have guided students in conducting corporate culture assessments for clients, at least one manager (often a CEO) believes he or she has an "open-door" policy where employees feel comfortable coming in to discuss anything that concerns them. When employees are asked about this, they will say that one or more aspects of the manager's communication style makes them feel uncomfortable and that they in fact don't believe that the manager has this "open-door" style. You often need an outsider to assess this for you and you may not like what you hear. Listen anyway.

SERVICE

Healthcare organizations are not unlike many other organizations in the factors that contribute to their culture. One thing that does, however, make it somewhat easier to foster the development of a strong culture is that many people who choose to work in this industry do so because of a desire to give service. This service-oriented mentality of healthcare workers can be used to its fullest advantage by managers. If your communication style is open and honest, and you share a service ethic with these workers, it may be easier to use this as the starting point for a shared vision. This shared vision in healthcare, communicated well to employees and other internal groups such as medical staff, can contribute to a healthy culture that fosters enhanced morale, increased productivity, and goal achievement.

YOUR INTERNAL AUDIENCE

The types of people who work in health-related organizations today have changed. Indeed, this is a reflection of the changes in the overall workforce since the 1950s. Generally, the work force in North America now is more highly educated, more cynical, more insecure and, as a result, more territorial. They are children of the television era and, increasingly, world-wide computer technology. They take less at face value and are much more difficult to mislead. There are more women (especially in healthcare delivery) and there is a more diverse multicultural representation. All of these factors have conspired to alter the way managers must think about the way they communicate. Even the use of non-sexist, inclusive language, an unknown issue just a generation ago, is an important communication result of these changes.

If we examine the changes in the nursing profession over the past half-century, we can see a striking example of just such a phenomenon. In 1960, American nurse Peggy Nuttal wrote a book titled *Nursing as a Career*[4] to provide potential nurses with career information. She begins her discussion of nursing by describing the personal characteristics that make for a suitable nursing candidate: "Without a doubt, the first and most important characteristic of a good nurse is that she should like people." Later she lists other favored characteristics such as a sense of humor, reliability, being good with your hands, and being fit. These are all probably good ideas (for anyone in a health profession) even today, but it is more likely that the

American and Canadian Nurses' associations might suggest that she or he should be bright, articulate, assertive, empathetic, and politically aware. This is a far cry from how Florence Nightingale saw nurses in 1881 when she suggested that "to be a good nurse one must be a good woman . . . What makes a good woman is the better or higher or holier nature: quietness . . . gentleness . . . patience . . . endurance . . . forbearance."

The reality is that when you look at the nurses sitting across from you at the union bargaining table, patience may or may not be one of the virtues you encounter, but quietness and gentleness are not likely to be in great abundance. You need to communicate with these women and men differently than your predecessors did. Knowing your audience is half the battle.

PRESSURES

Pressures on the healthcare system have changed the outlook of many health professionals with whom you will communicate. These pressures, such as litigation, insurance issues, and increasing consumer demands, have made many healthcare workers, particularly physicians, wary of anything that smacks of bureaucracy. As a healthcare manager at any level, you represent this. Communicating with wary groups of health professionals requires an empathetic attitude and skills that enable you to tailor your message and approach to an understanding of where they are coming from.

TECHNOLOGY

Another factor that you must consider in your communication with health professionals is the effect that increasing technology has had on their ranks. As medical technology has advanced over the past half century, so too have the numbers of specialized allied health professions required to work with these new technologies. For example, before the advent of ultrasonography, there were no sonography technicians; before open-heart surgery and dialysis, there were no perfusionists. Add to this the move to enhance the responsibilities of nurses with some procedures previously only performed by doctors, and you blur the lines of responsibility and increase the potential for turf wars. It is within this climate that you as a manager must communicate with other health professionals.

VOLUNTEERS

Volunteers are another group that a healthcare manager needs to communicate with on a regular basis. Many healthcare organizations rely on volunteers in working toward the organization's goal. In smaller, non-profit groups, volunteers may be the life-blood without which you cannot survive. For other, larger institutions, volunteers may have a more specific role, such as in fund-raising. Whatever role they play in your own organization, they are an important part of the internal audience, but they are not the same as paid employees. They need at all times to feel rewarded in other ways than monetary—and this morale boosting should color the tone of all communication that management has with volunteers. This should be your communication theme.

YOUR BOARD

One of the most important internal audiences that you have is your board. If you are, or at some point in your career will be, at a senior level in healthcare administration, then communicating with your board is an important issue. We will discuss this in detail in the next chapter.

Knowing as much as you can about your audience allows you to develop a communication style that is more likely to be accepted by that audience. Your messages, channels, and tone will be audience-specific.

COMMUNICATING INTERNALLY

Once you have acknowledged that you are communicating on a daily basis with diverse internal audiences (who should share a common vision), you need to examine the purpose of this communication and the approaches you will use.

As we have discussed previously, there are essentially only two general categories of communication. You are either engaged in one-way communication where the messages originate with you and the process is over when the message has been received by the audience, or two-way communication wherein you consider and act on feedback from your audience in response to your first communication.

An overall style categorized by one-way communication is considered to be a closed approach. Overuse of one-way communication by managers contributes to a weak culture with all its concomitant negative consequences. One-way techniques, used in conjunction with other approaches (where your employees and other staff already recognize that they have other opportunities for feedback), are sometimes the most efficient ways to convey information. You provide the information that the internal group needs.

There are, however, many reasons why you communicate with internal groups and most of them require two-way methods. You should be thinking constantly about how to open a dialogue and deal with the feedback that is to come.

Persuasion is sometimes a goal in your communication. You may need to have internal groups on-side for changes that are coming. You may need to persuade them to management's point of view.

Often, the purpose of your communication will be to build morale. In fact, you might want to consider that you are either contributing to enhanced morale or detracting from it every time you communicate. Examine your memos, your message in the newsletter, your e-mail correspondence, and your demeanor at meetings and presentations. Do they all have a positive component for internal groups? If not, you will need to change the tone of your messages. It is always possible to enhance morale, even when conveying negative news, if you consider your tone, the subliminal message underlying your words, and your presentation. And never forget that every time you walk down a hall, employees will draw conclusions from your non-verbal behavior. You are on display all the time.

COMMUNICATING WITH PATIENTS

Whether you refer to those served by your organization as patients (hospitals), clients (clinics), or residents (long-term care), these people are an important internal group while they are receiving services. Managers in health-related organizations need to feel comfortable communicating with these groups for a variety of reasons.

The most important reason is that patients who perceive that they have been listened to are happier patients. A fair amount of research supports the contention that patients who believe they have a positive relationship with their healthcare providers are less likely to take legal action against an individual or institution. It is important to provide high-quality, competent services, but the communication environment and the relationships that develop as a result are also vital.[5]

While the obvious health benefits of calm, satisfied patients seems to be an important enough reason to ensure that communication with patients is high quality, avoiding litigation is one that cannot be ignored either.

Depending upon your administrative level, you will have varying numbers of direct contacts with patients. As a senior administrator, you may hear from patients and their families only when there is either a problem or when they want to pay your organization a compliment. At lower levels, you may have day-to-day, face-to-face contact. Your level will determine the amount and method of communication, but the importance is the same at all levels.

Most organizations should consider conducting patient/client satisfaction surveys from time to time, ensuring that a large portion of the survey deals with the perceived communication competence of the organization.

HOSPITAL JARGON: GOOD OR BAD?

Several different kinds of jargon color the verbal communication in healthcare institutions. First, there is the medical terminology. While it is a necessary part of the communication between health professionals, such terminology can interfere with accurate message receipt by patients and their families. Health professionals at the individual level must learn to deal with this, ensuring that excessive medical terminology doesn't creep into their communication with patients or clients without explanation. Then there are all the acronyms and abbreviations that make their way into verbal and written communication. Ensuring that your communication with patients is not peppered with them can be a challenge.

There is also what I like to call secret medical "in-talk." If you spend any time around house staff (in teaching hospitals in particular), you hear this jargon. It is not always complimentary, but it is part of the hospital culture. Usually, health professionals use these expressions when talking to one another, and they are generally quite careful not to use this terminology around patients. In fact, American folklore researchers believe that sometimes these expressions are used by health professionals to actively conceal information from patients[6] (like the parent who spells something out in front of a young child).

The most widely recognized example of this is the term GOMER. If you are familiar with Samuel Shem's irreverent medical novel *The House of God*, you may recognize it. The term is usually used to refer to elderly, male patients, often chronically alcoholic, who arrive in the emergency room on a rather regular basis. But it has a number of interpretations, one of which is that it stands for "get out of my emergency room." Ask any emergency room physician if he or she has heard it.

Another acronym that has gained popularity over the years is FLK. It stands specifically for "funny looking kid" and is used to refer quickly to a child that at first glance doesn't look quite right but there hasn't yet been time for a diagnosis. It allows for the examining health professional to flag the unusual look of the child, often a newborn, so that time can be taken later to assess for problems. It is not meant for the patient. In fact, a recent news story in Canada reported that a mother was offended when she happened to see this written about her child and she threatened to sue for defamation (it turned out that the child did, indeed, have a medical problem). There have been no further developments on this case in the media, but it points to an important issue.

Healthcare organizations have their own jargon for communication with one another, but the health workers who use these terms need to be careful about how and when they use them. They are never appropriate messages to convey to patients. As a manager, it is your responsibility to be a communication role model by encouraging your staff to speak and communicate appropriately, especially around patients.

THE HOSPITAL GRAPEVINE

Is it a real communication method? You bet it is, and one that shouldn't be ignored. Most organizations, unless they are one-person operations, have a grapevine of some sort or another.

Public relations expert Fraser Seitel considers the grapevine to be one of the most powerful means of communication within an organization and quotes an employee publication that described it this way:

It's faster than a public address announcement and more powerful than a general instruction. It's able to leap from L.A. to San Francisco in a single bound. And its credibility is almost beyond Walter Cronkite's.[7]

When a rumor gains steam, it is almost impossible to stop, and you will almost never figure out who started it. Another PR expert believes that the attractiveness of the grapevine is a function of the fact that it is so heady. The truth and facts are much duller. Furthermore, "E-mail makes the grapevine work with the speed of electrons on copper wire or the speed of light over the fiber-optic network!"[8]

So, how do you deal with the grapevine? First, stay tuned in to it. It is a fact of life and can be an effective means of communicating information. Second, be prepared to correct any misconstrued information before it causes a problem within the ranks of your employees, volunteers, medical staff, and board. The grapevine is a wide-spreading entity and can even reach out and touch the community and the media.

Just remember two things: (1) the grapevine is always going to be there; and (2) employees prefer to receive information from official sources.

CREDIBILITY VERSUS FULL DISCLOSURE

Although this issue of credibility is not specific to internal communication, it is a particularly important issue at this juncture. Clearly, truth in managerial communication is key to the manager's credibility and is a value to be pursued. There is, however, another perspective that needs consideration. That comes from answering the questions: How much disclosure is enough to be truthful? How much is too much?

Open communication doesn't necessarily mean telling everything. Public relations consultant Diana Morris reports on a situation with one of her clients, a revered and prosperous community hospital that was dealing with merger offers one after another by refusing all of them. From a communication perspective, the hospital administration prided themselves in openness and frankness, telling everything about the offers and their adamant refusal to merge.

Finally, pressures on hospitals being what they were in the 1990s, they finally accepted one of the offers and merged with another hospital. The hospital brought in a communications consultant when they perceived that there may have been problems with the way their communication was handled. The consultant discovered that employees were very negative. They had lost all faith in the credibility of management communication because they had been told so much about how the hospital would not merge that turned out differently. As one employee put it, "Why do they always contradict themselves? As far as I am concerned, communication at this hospital has no credibility."[9]

This is a striking case in support of the notion that, despite all good intentions for honesty and openness in communication, telling employees everything is unnecessary and can be damaging. This means that great care and judgment must be exercised in making these decisions. What to tell, what not to tell, how much to tell, and when, are not in opposition to honesty.

KEY POINTS

1. Employees prefer important information to come directly from their supervisors in face-to-face encounters.

2. Your relationships with key internal groups such as employees, medical staff, volunteers, and your board are significantly affected by your ability to communicate with them.

3. The culture or climate of the organization is significantly affected by managerial communication style.

4. A healthcare organization with a weak culture is more likely to have difficulty meeting its goals.

5. You may not be the best judge of how your communication style is perceived by employees.

6. Internal audiences have changed in significant ways over the past 50 years and your understanding of these characteristics is crucial to your ability to communicate.

7. In every communication encounter you have with internal groups or individuals, you are either contributing to or detracting from morale.

8. Patients or clients in healthcare institutions are less likely to take legal action against organizations and/or individuals who they believe have communicated well with them.

9. Never ignore the hospital grapevine.

10. Honesty in internal communication is not synonymous with full disclosure.

NOTES

1. Foehrenbach, J. and S. Goldfarb. 1990. "Employee Communication in the '90's: Greater Expectations," *IABC Communication World*, May-June.
2. *New Illustrated Webster's Dictionary of the English Language*. 1992. New York: PMC Publishing Company, Inc., p. 241.

3. "Reputation Management: I Believe." 1998. Http://www.prcentral.com/rmmj97j&j.htm.
4. Nuttal, P. 1960. *Nursing as a Career*. London: B.T. Botsford.
5. Ray, E. and K. Miller. 1990. "Communication in Health-Care Organizations," in *Communication and Health: Systems and Applications*, E. Ray and L. Donohew (eds), Hillsdale, NJ: Lawrence Erlbaum and Associates, Publishers, pp. 92–107.
6. George, V. and A. Duns. 1978. "The GOMER: A Figure of American Hospital Fold Speech,"*Journal of American Folklore* 91, 568–581.
7. Seitel, F. 1995. *The Practice of Public Relations*, 6th ed. Englewood Cliffs, NJ: Prentice Hall, p. 320.
8. Cutlip, S., A. Center and G. Broom. 2000. *Effective Public Relations*, 8th ed. Upper Saddle River, NJ: Prentice Hall, p. 297.
9. Morris, D. 1999. "Less is More: The Case Against Open Communication," *Journal of Employee Communication Management*, March-April, p. 10.

FOR YOUR BOOKSHELF . . .

Seitel, Fraser P. 1995. *The Practice of Public Relations.* 6th ed. Prentice Hall.

ON THE WEB . . .

"Growing the Corporate Culture"
http://www.smartbix.com/sbs/arts/ste9.htm

Ragan Communications, Journal of Employee Communication Management
http://www.ragan.com

7

Wooing Your Board

Three people were at work on a construction site. All were doing the same job, but when each was asked what the job was, the answers varied. "Breaking rocks," the first replied. "Earning my living," the second said. "Helping to build a cathedral," said the third.

— Peter Schultz

WE ALL SEE things from our own point of view. Boards, however, often seem to have more than one perspective from which to interpret the world.

If you think about it, your board is really a hybrid of your internal and external communities; although when it comes to having their "say" on organizational matters, they are firmly entrenched (at least in their minds) insiders. Perhaps you see them differently. Figure 7.1 provides a visual illustration of where the interfaces are and where the pressures on the relationship originate.

The fragility of the relationship between board and management can stem from the simple truth that you are on the inside every day and they are not. Therein lie both their strength and their weakness.

Being on the outside looking in provides an oft-needed objective eye. When you are so close that you can't see the forest for

115

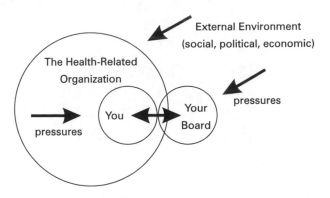

the trees, it can help to have strong rapport with a group one step removed. Further, this external view provides important input that may reflect where their other foot is planted—namely the external community. That external input coming from a group that has a vested interest in what you are doing is valuable.

On the other hand, as many healthcare managers have learned from hard experience, boards sometimes can't quite grasp the rhyme and reason of what are now the realities of today's healthcare industry. In healthcare, perhaps more than in any other industry, self-identification can cloud the reasoning of even the most level-headed board member. The emotion and value-laden characteristics of healthcare sometimes make that highly regarded objectivity a fleeting commodity.

Therefore, the relationship between administration and board, fueled as it is by communication processes, can be a challenging one. However, being strategic about communication with your board can go a long way toward building a mutually beneficial relationship and your own credibility.

THE POWER OF YOUR BOARD

"Most affairs of American life are controlled or influenced by boards."[1] This is the opening line in Cyril O. Houle's book

Governing Boards, and a scary one at that. Houle goes on to give us chapter and verse about the kinds of groups who sit around "boardrooms" (they *are* everywhere, aren't they?) and make decisions that affect our lives. He lists churches, governments, private corporations, educational institutions, professional organizations, trade unions, not-for-profits, and, of course, healthcare organizations, to name a few.

Could your organization accomplish its goals without a board? Think very carefully about your answer. Your positive or negative response is likely to be directly correlated to the quality of your own personal relationship with your board. Whether you believe that they are effective or not, they do have a degree of power that is a reflection of the trust (hence the term trustees) that your community has in your board's role in protecting their interests. A wise administrator respects that public trust and recognizes the image power that a board has. This alone makes strategic communication with your board vital—not for the purpose of controlling them, but for developing a rapport with them.

COMMUNICATING WITH A PURPOSE

It may seem self-evident why you need to communicate with your board. But if you consider this just another part of your managerial duties, you have missed the point of recognizing the importance of strategic communication. There should never be an encounter between you or your managers and your board that is not purposeful and well considered.

INFORM

The first strategic purpose of communication with your board is a result of their view of themselves as insiders. They have informational needs. Thus, your goal is to *inform*. What you inform them about, to what extent, and when are strategic considerations.

Board members need information about:

- background on issues that they will consider as part of their role as board members.
- actions taken by administration that are likely to be made known publicly.
- any new or unusual occurrences that are being made public through the media.

Essentially, your board members need enough information to do their jobs and to feel that they are important insiders. In addition to this, because they are important external ambassadors of your organization, they need to be "kept in the loop" about issues that are or will be of a public nature. There is nothing more irritating for a board member than to hear about an organization's activities in the news or from a neighbor. If you want to incite them to riot, just treat them with less consideration than you do your employees.

Obviously, *your* opinion about how much information they need to do their jobs may differ from *their* opinions about how much information they need. In addition, there are likely to be differing perspectives on this issue from one board member to another. This is why a good personal relationship with the board chair can be helpful. Your own interpersonal skills are called into play in the development of your relationship.

A good board chair who understands administration's point of view (although he or she might not always agree with it) can be a formidable ally in your quest to woo your board. Cultivating this interpersonal relationship can be a key element in your ability to communicate your messages effectively to your board.

PERSUADE

The second important purpose for communication with your board is to *persuade* them about issues for which, from your perspective at least, you need their support. One of the most important aspects of persuasion when dealing with your board is to ensure that you tailor your message specifically to this audience. It will not be effective enough to simply use the same approach that you use for this issue with clients and the community, or even your employees for that matter. You need to think very carefully about packaging the persuasive message for your board. This may mean thinking about each individual's perspective as you prepare for any presentation of a persuasive nature.

PACKAGING YOUR COMMUNICATION

Just as important as purpose and message when communicating with your board, so too are when and how you do it.

WHEN

The first rule of *when* to communicate with your board is to do it regularly. And this does not mean only at scheduled board meetings. You need a vehicle for direct communication between the highest levels of administration in your organization and all board members between board meetings. If your organization is of any size at all, you need to put this in writing.

Figure 7.2 is an example of a monthly, written communication vehicle whose objectives are to:

- nurture your relationship with each board member;
- inform them of information in a timely fashion; and
- cultivate within them a feeling of belonging to your organization.

HOW

From these objectives comes the content. Consider each of these objectives to ensure that any material you send achieves

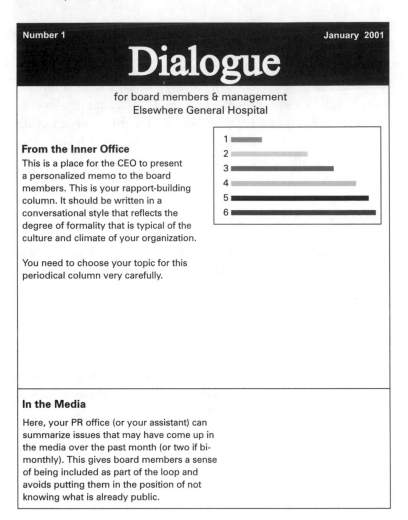

Dialogue

for board members & management
Elsewhere General Hospital

From the Inner Office

This is a place for the CEO to present a personalized memo to the board members. This is your rapport-building column. It should be written in a conversational style that reflects the degree of formality that is typical of the culture and climate of your organization.

You need to choose your topic for this periodical column very carefully.

In the Media

Here, your PR office (or your assistant) can summarize issues that may have come up in the media over the past month (or two if bi-monthly). This gives board members a sense of being included as part of the loop and avoids putting them in the position of not knowing what is already public.

each one, every time. Following are some suggestions for the kind of materials that would help to move you toward your goals:

- a monthly message from the CEO and/or other managers
- a media monitor with explanatory notes as necessary

- a calendar of internal events as well as external events that your organization may be participating in

This newsletter-type communication should come not from your public relations staff, but from you. The advantage of this format over a letter or memo is its perceived level of professionalism. Then comes the question of distribution.

Should you distribute this kind of communication electronically? It depends on:

1. the extent to which electronic communication is valued by your board members (not by you);
2. the accessibility of electronic distribution to all board members (not just the majority); and
3. the board members' opinions about receiving this kind of information from you in electronic format (this means you have to ask them).

If you decide to distribute this electronically, you should add a photo of yourself to personalize it, and lay it out in just as visually attractive a manner as you would if it were printed. If you are not familiar with the implications of reading text on-screen you should seek help from your public relations department or consultant.

Obviously, if you do not distribute the newsletter electronically, you will have to mail it. Board members should be asked their preference for receiving mail at home or at their place of business. Do not hand it out at board meetings. This defeats your purpose of enhancing the number of communication encounters you have with your board.

Board–administration communication can often be a special challenge for healthcare managers. If you share a vision and a set of core values, however, communication will at least have a common ground from which to start. After that it is up to you.

Your personal skills in communication are essential to both you and your organization.

KEY POINTS

1. The main goal of strategic communication with your board is to enhance your rapport and the relationship that emanates from it.

2. The goal of communication with your board is not to control them.

3. Two important objectives for communication encounters with board members are to inform and to persuade.

4. The first rule of management–board communication is to do it regularly.

5. The second rule of management–board communication is to have a specific vehicle for doing it.

6. Your own personal skills in interpersonal and written communication as well as your ability to make presentations are key to successful management–board communication.

NOTES

1. Houle, C. 1997. *Governing Boards: Their Nature and Nurture.* San Francisco: Jossey-Bass, p. 1.

FOR YOUR BOOKSHELF . . .

Houle, Cyril. 1997. *Governing Boards: Their Nature and Nurture.* *Jossey-Bass Publishers.*

8

Working With Public Relations

Alone we can do so little; together we can do so much.

— Helen Keller

"BRING IN THE PR people!"

It seems like a familiar refrain. When have you heard those infamous words? Does it happen when things are going smoothly? Or have you more frequently heard them when something within your organization has gone wrong or is about to go wrong? Strikes, sexual harassment charges, lawsuits, medical malpractice — these are just a few of the unpleasant situations that can plague a healthcare manager and send you rushing to the PR people before the media are on your doorstep.

If you are working within a large enough organizational structure, you are probably fortunate to have a public relations staff. But do you really use them to their fullest advantage? Do you even know what they are capable of doing for your organization? One of the most important parts of healthcare communication on a macro level (beyond you as the individual communicator) is the public relations function of your department or organization. If you are part of a small organization that does not have the luxury of such specialized communication staff, then you are it.

In this chapter we will examine what modern public relations practice can be expected to accomplish and look at the difference between PR and marketing, as well as the similarities between the skills required for PR and fundraising. In the end, you should be able to assess the public relations function in your organization or department and use their expertise to your best advantage.

WHO "THEY" ARE AND WHAT "THEY" DO

It would be derelict of anyone writing about healthcare communication to neglect a specific discussion of healthcare public relations. In general terms, modern public relations is the strategic application of communications tools and techniques to help organizations develop and maintain relationships. Public relations requires practitioners who have managerial and technical skills, creativity, integrity, and flexibility. Indeed, most modern PR people consider public relations to be a managerial function, and broadly speaking, it is in the best interests of an organization to consider public relations in this context. There are, however, both managerial and technical levels to public relations and it is useful for other managers to understand these two levels.

RELATIONSHIPS

Before we can differentiate between these two levels, it is important for healthcare managers to understand something about *relationships*. We have discussed them in specific situations up to this point, but let's take a step back for a moment to consider their broader context.

The two most important aspects of an organization's relationships—both internal and external—are as follows:

- The development and nurturing of strong, long-term relationships with a variety of publics is key to any organization's image and identity, public goodwill, and ultimate ability to achieve its mission.
- Communication with these publics, whether that communication is intentional, unintentional, proactive, or reactive is what builds those relationships.

Your own communication skills as a manager contribute in a large way to the development of those relationships, whether at the departmental or organizational level.

Consider a manager at the lower levels of a hospital hierarchy. This manager likely has direct contact with patients and thus can have considerable effect on the development of that hospital's external image. A manager at this level whose communication skills are well honed can leave a very positive image of that organization with patients or clients who are likely to talk about the organization positively to outsiders. This helps to build positive relationships with the community.

A CEO can also have the same kind of effects on a higher level of the hierarchy. Make no mistake, however—regardless of your managerial level in a health-related organization, your own skills and strategic understanding of communication will have effects, intended or not, on the relationships that both you and your organization build with a variety of publics.

PR TECHNICIANS

Public relations practitioners see themselves in two ways. First are PR technicians. These individuals are trained in the development of communication tools and techniques that can be applied to the implementation of a plan that they may or may not have been involved in developing. For example, a PR technician writes news releases and designs and writes newsletters, annual reports, brochures, promotional video scripts—in short, the technician carries out many of the activities that have been planned by the communication management team of the organization.

PR MANAGERS

PR managers—in addition to the technical work that may be required of them from time to time—also develop the strategic communication plan for the organization and manage the human and other resource aspects of the implementation of the plan. In the real world of small public relations departments, these people may be one and the same, although some PR technicians are better equipped than others to carry out the managerial aspects of a higher-level position. For example, someone trained in journalism is likely to make a very good PR technician, but unless that individual's education is supplemented by a serious dose of mentoring in public relations planning, he or she will probably lack the knowledge and skills to be a PR manager.

WHAT PR OFFERS

What then, specifically, does the public relations function have to offer healthcare organizations? It can

- assist the organization in the development of a healthy public image so that even during times of crisis, the organization is likely to get a fair hearing.
- work with the management of the organization to develop strategies for handling many kinds of potential problems.
- help prepare for media encounters and assist you with your writing/editing/speaking engagements.
- support the marketing of your services (including conferences and events) if that is part of what you require (more about the marketing function later).

Many people outside the public relations field see public relations as synonymous with publicity. While the generation of publicity is a part of the one-way communication function that any good public relations person can do well, it is only a very small part. While generation of publicity is often a good thing, not all publicity is positive for the organization. Thus, even potentially publicity-generating activities must be carefully considered within an overall plan for managing the organization's relationships.

With all this emphasis on public relations as a management function, it should be clear to any healthcare manager that today's public relations people are better used as fire-preventers than fire-fighters. In other words, don't wait until there is a crisis before bringing in the PR people.

PUBLIC RELATIONS OR MARKETING?

Marketing has become a fact of life for most organizations involved in healthcare, whether they like it or not. By definition, marketing means selling a service or product to a customer, the hallmark of which is an exchange of some sort, usually money for the purchase of the goods or service. As public relations authors Scott Cutlip, Allen Center, and Glen Broom say, "The hospital industry is increasingly embroiled in public policy debates and aggressively pursuing patients."[1] This pursuit of patients has resulted in the requirement for a marketing effort of some kind. Isn't public relations just a part of the marketing plan? Clearly not. But they work beautifully together.

We have already established that public relations is responsible for the nurturing of long-term relationships with a variety of publics, all of whose good will are important to the successful achievement of the healthcare organization's mission. This is not the same as marketing, but the two are, indeed, related.

Traditionally, marketing and public relations used to be differentiated by the simple exhortation that marketing sells goods and services, while public relation sells the organization. This definition is far too simplistic and fails to recognize that modern public relations practice often finds itself in the uncomfortable position of having to advise management that they need to be honest about their shortcomings—hardly what one would term "selling" the organization—to fulfill their obligation to the greater good.

Another way of differentiating between PR and marketing has been to indicate that marketers use advertising (paid, controlled media), while PR uses publicity (free, uncontrolled media). This is certainly no longer true as marketers have recognized the marketing value of some of these public relations techniques and PR has increasingly turned to paid advertising to control the message.

The best way to think about the differences between these two external communications functions is to consider the kind of relationship that is the objective of each. Marketers seek to develop a relationship with current and potential customers/clients/patients so that the services offered by that particular organization are selected by the customer/client/patient when the need to purchase arises. Thus, this short-term, in-the-moment relationship is key. Eventually, the marketers might be interested in maintenance of these customers, but when you come right down to it, the relationship at that moment of decision is all-important.

Public relations, on the other hand, seeks to develop and nurture long-term relationships with a variety of publics so that the organization's positive reputation allows it to accomplish a variety of objectives, not just selling services. For example, positive public relations provides for the greater likelihood of fair coverage by media, for community support in ventures such as expansion, for employee buy-in of mergers and acquisitions, for attracting high-quality medical and allied health staff, for positive relationships with funders, and for decreasing the likelihood of litigation. Positive public relations also supports the marketing effort of the organization by creating a climate of goodwill that allows potential customers/clients/patients to emerge from the community. Marketing can then take over.

Marketing of healthcare services, however, differs in several important ways from the marketing of other goods and services. Most healthcare executives are well aware of these differences.

- The individual (or group) actually paying for the services is often not the person selecting the service provider (i.e., insurance companies have limited control over selection and cost decisions).
- The nature and location of that service are generally not controlled by the person receiving the service (i.e., physicians make the recommendations).
- Healthcare services are often unpleasant for the purchaser.[2]

Thus, long-term relationships with physicians and insurers are just as important as the long-term relationships with clients.

Healthcare organizations today need both public relations and marketing to function optimally. They work together, but conceptually, they are two different communication functions.

PUBLIC RELATIONS AND FUNDRAISING

There is a natural relationship between public relations and fundraising. For non-profit healthcare organizations, fundraising is often crucial to their operation, and fundraising is nothing if not a communication activity. How do these two fall together?

In many smaller organizations, public relations and development are not only the same department, but often use the skills and services of the same individuals. Obviously, an organization cannot raise funds successfully if it has a poor public image. Thus, the relationships that public relations builds are fundamental to fundraising. Once that image is nurtured, then a fundraising case needs to be communicated to the target potential donors. Public relations' communication expertise must be utilized in this exercise as well. To summarize:

> Public relations representatives participate directly in fundraising by organizing and conducting solicitation programs, or they serve as consultants to specialized development departments of their organizations. Organizations often employ professional firms to conduct their campaigns on a fee basis. In that case, the organization's public relations representatives usually have a liaison function.[3]

It would be impossible to conduct a fundraising campaign of any sort without communicating your messages skillfully to your target donors. Thus, for a non-profit organization, formal public relations expertise is crucial.

IF YOU DON'T HAVE A PR STAFF

If you are a manager in a small organization that does not have the luxury of professional communicators on staff, then you are "it." Your best strategy is to ferret out as many communications and public relations professionals in your community as you can and beg them to help you set up a volunteer PR committee, staffed with people who possess the required expertise. This group can become the core of experts that you use to develop a plan for public relations and to train you and your staff. The training should consist of helping everyone in your organization to understand the importance of public relations and its relationship to the success of your organization. The training should also help managers to hone their communication skills.

In addition to these functions, your volunteer public relations consultants can also provide you with considerable technical expertise as you develop and use specific tools such as news releases, brochures, annual reports, and media kits.

Take advantage of every opportunity you have to attend professional development seminars presented by the organizations to which communicators belong. Some web sites listed at the end of this chapter can guide you to your local chapters.

It is extremely important for managers in healthcare organizations, whether they have professional public relations help or not, to familiarize themselves with the roles and functions of a public relations staff. To neglect this is to neglect an important part of your overall strategy for accomplishing your organizational goals.

USING OUTSIDE PR CONSULTANTS

In these times of increasing outsourcing, many high-ranking executives have determined that it is best to outsource their public relations and communication activities. However, because healthcare organizations have some very specific needs, hiring outside help for all PR activities is not always the best choice.

Healthcare requires individuals with certain sensitivities to issues such as client confidentiality and an appreciation that the services provided by that organization are frequently unpleasant for those clients. Having in-house staff allows a healthcare organization to select communicators with the personal philosophies that are consistent with the mission of the organization. In addition, from the perspective of other health professionals within the organization, someone from the outside is likely to be viewed with some suspicion. Thus, whenever financially feasible, it is always in the best interests of a healthcare organization to have its own public relations staff. There are, however, times when even an organization with a well-staffed PR function must, or at least should, hire out-side consultants.

Here are several different scenarios where an outside public relations consultant would be beneficial and even preferable to internal staff:

- When you have specific communication activities that need to be accomplished and *insufficient staff*. For example, your staff might be completely capable of organizing a large event such as an open house or a fundraising dinner, but they may not have the human resources to do so.
- When the communications task is *outside the area of your internal staff's expertise*. If you are merging with another healthcare institution, it may be preferable to hire outside communications consultants who have been through such a situation with other organizations. They are more likely to be able to anticipate public relations problems (especially ones with your internal groups) before they arise.
- When you need to *assess the quality of your current public relations programming*. Part of a high-quality public relations function is the necessity for evaluation of outcomes. Hiring an outside consultant every three to five years to conduct a public relations audit is a very wise idea. While any competent PR practitioner can audit his or her own department's function, this person can't be relied upon for objectivity. An outside perspective can be extremely valuable as you move toward new goals.

While this is not the place for a detailed discussion of how to hire a public relations consultant, there are some tips that can be helpful. Keep in mind that there are similarities in hiring any kind of outside consultant, and your past experience in hiring others is applicable in this situation. The following are some questions that may assist you in beginning your search.

- *What services do they offer?*
  - media relations and/or training
  - government relations
  - lobbying
  - employee communications
  - client relations
  - investor relations
  - donor relations
  - issues management
  - crisis communication
  - community relations
  - print media development
  - broadcast media development[4]
- *What size of organization have they worked with in the past?* One size does not fit all. If you are part of a small, long-term care facility, their experience with large, tertiary care hospitals may not provide them with the kind of background that you need.
- *What types of organizations have they worked with in the past?* A public relations consultant who has never worked with a healthcare organization is not a good fit for you. There would be a steep learning curve for a consultant who is not familiar with the external and internal environments of healthcare. In addition, if you are a non-profit organization, does the consultant have experience with non-profits?
- *Where are they physically located?* Do they have a geographic presence in your community? If they don't, you need to assess the amount and kind of personal, face-to-face contact that will be necessary for you and to meet the expectations of your staff. If you have a choice to use local consultants or ones from afar, you are usually better to use local.
- *Can they provide you with a list of past clients?* If you see any personal contacts on their list, call those first. Listen to

what your contacts are saying and what they are not saying. If you don't see any contacts, look for other healthcare organizations whose administrators you know are a part of a professional organization to which you belong. Failing that, cold call those who seem to represent similar kinds of organizations to your own.

Public relations consultants can provide much-needed expertise to individual healthcare executives and their organizations. They can even be cost-effective. Public relations in healthcare, however, is a necessary internal requirement.

YOUR PR FUNCTION: HOW DOES IT MEASURE UP?

A well-functioning public relations department, even if it consists of only one person, needs to be assessed from time to time. Knowing the questions to ask makes this assessment much easier. Here are the questions that you need to ask regularly.

1. Is your PR staff at the boardroom table?
2. Are they doing environmental scanning (i.e., gathering data about the external environment)?
3. Do you receive regular reports of the results of this scanning?
4. Do you approve an operational PR plan at least annually?
5. Do they have a good grasp of healthcare and how it is organized?
6. Do you receive a media monitoring report each month?
7. Are your policies for clearance (e.g., who has to approve news releases, etc.) clear, efficient, and used at all times?
8. Does your PR staff evaluate its activities on a regular basis?

If you answered no to any of these questions, then you have a problem area within your PR function. You need to carefully examine how you are using your staff and consider how to fix the problems.

KEY POINTS

1. Modern public relations is the strategic application of communications tools and techniques to help organizations develop and manage their relationships with important internal and external groups.

2. Public relations is loosely divided by its technical and managerial functions—and healthcare organizations need both.

3. Generating publicity (a good example of one-way communication) is only a very small part of modern public relations.

4. Public relations and marketing are not the same thing; one is not subsumed by the other. They can work well together.

5. The nature of the changing healthcare environment has made it almost impossible for healthcare organizations to function well without both of these external communication functions.

6. Fundraising requires well-developed, well-targeted communication campaigns and thus can be considered within the domain of public relations in non-profit healthcare organizations.

7. If your organization is too small to have a separate public relations function, consider developing a volunteer board consisting of local public relations experts.

8. Public relations in healthcare is best practiced as an internal activity, but there are some specific occasions when you may require outside PR consultants.

NOTES

1. Cutlip, S., A. Center, and G. Broom. 2000. *Effective Public Relations*, 8th ed. Upper Saddle River, NJ: Prentice Hall, p. 530.
2. *Ibid.*
3. Wilcox, D., P. Ault, and W. Agee. 1998. *Public Relations: Strategies and Tactics*, 5th ed. New York: Addison Wesley Longman, Inc., p. 396.
4. Harris, T. 1992. *Choosing and Working With Your Public Relations Firm*. Lincolnwood, IL: NTC Business Books.

FOR YOUR BOOKSHELF . . .

Nelson, Joyce. 1989. *Sultans of Sleaze: Public Relations and the Media.* Between the Lines Press.

Newsom, Doug, Judy Vanslyke Turk, and Dean Kruckegberg. 1996. *This Is P.R.: The Realities of Public Relations.* Wadsworth Publishing Co.

Wilcox, Dennis, Phillip Ault and Warren Agee. 1998. *Public Relations Strategies and Tactics,* 5th ed. Addison Wesley Educational Publishers.

ON THE WEB . . .

American Medical Writers Association
http://www.amwa.org

Bibliography of Public Relations Literature
http://lamar.colostate.edu/~hallahan/articles.htm

Canadian Public Relations Society
http://www.cprs.ca

International Association of Business Communicators
http://www.iabc.com

Public Relations Society of America
http://www.prsa.org

LEVEL III

The World Outside

We are moving toward the top of our strategic pyramid. At the lowest, and broadest, level we examined your personal communication knowledge, attitudes, and skills as a healthcare manager. We then moved to the internal environment as a first strategic step in creating a healthy communication climate within your organization and solid relationships with a number of important internal groups. Our next level involves extending our sphere of concern and influence to outside the organization.

Healthcare organizations have a wide variety of possible outside audiences and publics. These external stakeholders whose goodwill is important to your organization include potential clients, other healthcare organizations in your community, your geographical neighborhood, funders, potential funders, and the media. It is possible to consider all of these as your "community." Level III, then, is devoted to developing lines of communication with your organization's community and, because of its considerable importance in communicating messages widely, the media.

Creating Community Relationships

Always do more than is required of you.

— George S. Patton

HOW MUCH ARE your community relations worth to you? How important are your own communication skills and public forays in the development of those relationships? If you are unsure about your answer to either of these questions, then be prepared for a wide variety of problems if you or your organization's relationship with your community is poor.

Poor community relationships can result in some or all of the following:

- poor reputation
- inability to compete
- inability to reach those who require your services
- inability to attract high-quality staff or volunteers
- lack of support for new initiatives
- negative media coverage

And these are just the start.

Unfortunately, many healthcare managers seem to think that the cultivation of community relations is someone else's responsibility. Some consider it to be an issue for their auxiliaries, while others rely completely on their public relations staff to deal with it. The bottom line is that solid community relations begin at the top, not the bottom.

WHAT IT MEANS TO BE PART OF A COMMUNITY

Generally, when we refer to our community we are referring to the geographic locality within which we live and work. But a community is also a collection of people with common interests and it is important to think about your community from both perspectives. It is not just that entity that you know as your town, city or municipality: it is the people who make that geographic entity more than bricks and mortar. They give it life. And your organization is a part of both.

Community relations has been defined in a number of different ways, but it depends on one simple understanding: institutions or organizations are interdependent.[1] Management's recognition that no organization is an island and that it needs outside support and sometimes guidance is fundamental to cultivating good community relationships. Further, interdependence means that each participant expects and needs things from the others. Unfortunately, healthcare organizations often mistakenly believe that they are special cases because their work is somehow on a higher moral ground than, say, a manufacturer. This is a dangerous misconception. Healthcare organizations need to achieve integration into their communities just as do other kinds of institutions. As Professor Warren Burkett points out, "All hospitals need to encourage community confidence in them, and to seek to do it through publicity about their successes, equipment, facilities, people, services, and patients."[2]

Another important issue to consider before we get to your own personal role in communication with your community is that of external control. If you are part of an organization that is part of a larger organization without headquarters in your community, then developing a rapport with your community can be an even more crucial challenge. Outside control of an organization, whether real or perceived, can be a source of conflict with the community if this relationship is not cultivated and nurtured.

YOUR PERSONAL ROLE

Managers at all levels in healthcare organizations must cultivate an awareness of their outside communities. Your own participation in the community and your personal communication skills can have a distinctly positive effect on your organization's relationship with its community.

Public opinion about your organization can be closely related to the communication style that is perceived by the public on many levels. For example, the communication style of the CEO comes directly across to the community in the way he or she responds to the media in crisis, as well as non-crisis, situations. In addition, the style can come across indirectly in the way the community perceives that management treats its employees. Good or bad, these issues can affect public opinion, with all of its implications.

WHAT YOUR COMMUNITY EXPECTS FROM YOU

Your community expects a variety of things from your organization.

- *It expects that you will do what you say you are doing (to "walk the talk" as it were).* If you have a publicly proclaimed mission, you need to be perceived to be doing just what that mission says you will do. If the public doesn't know what your mission is, then it is time to ask why, and what you can do to change that.
- *It expects that you will provide employment at a fair wage.* If you have continuing difficulties with your unions or are accused of unfair labor practices in any way, this will be detrimental to your organization's image. How you communicate about these issues, however, is just as important to the community's perception as the actual issues.
- *It expects you to look like a good community citizen.* The visual image you portray speaks volumes. Ill-kept buildings or facilities send unintended messages to your community.
- *It expects you to act like a good citizen.* For example, how do you dispose of your medical refuse? This is an important community issue where actions speak louder than words.
- *It expects you to participate in the life of the community.* Communities tend to make allowances for healthcare organizations because of the nature of the work done by the professionals and non-professionals on-site. However, community relations would be enhanced by participation in activities, especially health-related ones. Does your organization have a team in an annual fundraising run for a particular illness such as breast cancer or AIDS? It doesn't have to reflect directly your own mission, but will imply volumes to the community about your all-around concerns for the health and well-being of the citizens.
- *It expects you to communicate in a way it will understand.* This is particularly important if any part of your community is actually a sub-public that reflects a diversity in cultures—and this applies to almost every kind of health-related organization

there is. As one author on the topic of multicultural public relations points out, an organization's relationship with its community should be "inclusive, self-revealing, genuine, personal, and emergent."[3]

These expectations are reasonable and rational. Any organization that values its future will respond to these challenges positively.

CORPORATE SUPPORT

Non-profit, health-related organizations, whether they provide care, services, education, or research, are often on the other side when it comes to community relations programs. In other words, you may find yourself on the receiving end of a community relations effort that supports the public image of a profit-making corporation (such as a pharmaceutical company). Being a part of a corporation's strategic philanthropy program sounds like a win-win situation. Their image is enhanced, and your organization receives much-needed financial support, equipment, or professional expertise. But does this support *your* community relations? It depends on several factors.

The first factor to consider is the corporation's profile — not in its own eyes, but in those of your community. If the organization supporting your efforts has a particularly bad relationship with your community, you might consider doing some research with your own community leaders before partnering with that organization in any way. It could have implications for your own relationship with the community.

Another factor worth considering is whether the corporation's support comes with strings attached — or even when this could be perceived by any of your important stakeholders. It may be a matter of selling only that company's soft drinks on your premises, instead of their competitors', or they may require you to stock only their brand of a particular drug. In any case, can you and your relationships live with their conditions?

If you turn down corporate support for any reason, how will people (including both internal and external groups) perceive your actions? If you are the CEO of a hospital and a tobacco company offers a much-needed financial injection, can you accept it? Is it morally acceptable to take it? To turn it down? Are your communication skills (and those of other managers) up to the task of facing your employees, other donors, your board, your community, and the media?

Indeed, if a non-profit healthcare organization does become a part of a corporate philanthropy program, managers have roles to play, and these roles generally involve communication skills. You may be required to:

- appear at news conferences with corporate officials;
- give media interviews;
- speak at corporate functions;
- write articles in their company newsletters; or
- take part in a variety of social functions.

It is not a simple matter of saying yes!

WHAT YOU SHOULD BE DOING

Healthcare organizations use a wide variety of communication strategies to develop and enhance their relationships with their communities. The public image of healthcare has changed drastically. As the environment of health services has changed, the public has begun to view many healthcare organizations as part of just another huge, uncaring industry. Communicating with your community to ensure that they do not take this attitude toward your organization is crucial. Healthcare managers can play key roles if their own skills are well honed.

Here are some of the kinds of community relations programs that healthcare organizations develop and implement, in which healthcare managers can play a significant role.

- *Public information or social marketing campaigns.* While many of these programs relate to specific health concerns in which health professionals play significant roles as spokespersons, healthcare organizations have more recently become concerned about educational campaigns to help consumers navigate the system. Campaigns that focus on healthcare delivery are ideal situations for healthcare managers to get involved. Your involvement can go far beyond the planning of such campaigns—you might consider a role as a spokesperson.
- *Speakers bureaus.* Many healthcare organizations and facilities have a well-developed speakers bureau that provides speakers for community groups. Today's consumers and community members are acutely interested in the system as well as in health policy. Healthcare managers should be a part of this. You can select a topic area in which you are interested and to which you can bring some personal experience. The speakers bureau administrators (typically the PR department, but it could be anyone) organize the placement. If you don't have one, you might consider developing one.
- *Open Houses.* Many healthcare organizations occasionally open their doors to their community. This is a terrific opportunity to participate in an effort to help consumers understand the role of management in healthcare. Many managers place themselves in the background at these times, believing that the community is interested only in front-line health professionals. It doesn't have to be that way. As healthcare looms larger in the eyes of the community, it needs to see and hear that healthcare is not a faceless,

non-caring industry. Your participation can go a long way to help with this.

KEY POINTS

1. Poor relationships with your community can result in a variety of challenges, from a poor reputation (and all that results from that) to an inability to attract and keep good staff.

2. Communication between organizations and their communities is key to that relationship; healthcare managers play a pivotal role.

3. The general perception of healthcare is fast becoming one of a faceless, uncaring industry little different from any other service. Community relations can change that.

4. Your community has high expectations of your organization: that you walk the talk, provide employment at a fair wage, and participate within the community. They also expect your organization to both look and act like a good citizen and to communicate with them in a way they understand.

5. If you are part of a non-profit organization, be careful when the shoe is on the other foot and you are enticed to become part of a corporate strategic philanthropy endeavor.

6. Your own communication skills will be key when you are taking your part in community relations programs.

NOTES

1. Baskin, O., C. Aronoff, and D. Lattimore. 1997. *Public Relations: The Profession and the Practice*, 4th ed. Madison, WI: Brown & Benchmark.

2. Burkett, W. 1986. *News Reporting: Science, Medicine and High Technology*. Ames, IA: The Iowa State University Press, p. 105.
3. Banks, S. 1995. *Multicultural Public Relations: A Social-Interpretive Approach*. Thousand Oaks, CA: Sage Publications, p. 70.

FOR YOUR BOOKSHELF . . .

Banks, Stephen. 1995. *Multicultural Public Relations.* Sage.

ON THE WEB . . .

Boston College Center for Corporate Community Relations
http://www.bc.edu/bc__org/avp/csom/executive/ccr/frames/html

The Finley Hospital (Dubuque, IA) Community Relations
http://www.finleyhospital.org/comm__rel.htm

Communicating With the Media

Four hostile newspapers are more to be feared than a
thousand bayonets.

— Napoleon Bonaparte

"NOWHERE ELSE ARE the threads of scientific enterprise
more tangled with economic, political, personality, and social
values than in medicine and the related health sciences."[1] When
Professor Warren Burkett wrote these words in his 1986 book
News Reporting: Science, Medicine and High Technology, he was
reflecting a trend of the 1980s, a trend that has continued into the
new century. Medicine and healthcare are news—in fact, they
are big news. As a result, anyone involved in the management of
healthcare facilities or services is likely to find that involvement
with the media is an inevitable part of getting the job done—a
part that cannot be ignored.

Medicine is front-page news. Not a day goes by without
some news of a medical drama, or healthcare and the economy,
or healthcare and politics. Medical news does, indeed, have
everything that makes for a good news story: human interest,

science, personalities, politics, economics, and social values. And with the increasingly blurred lines between information and entertainment—what some commentators refer to these days as "infotainment"—healthcare stories play well, as they say in the media. While the numbers vary slightly from study to study, it is widely believed that somewhere in the vicinity of 40 percent of what appears in newspapers is medically related.[2] Add to that number the array of television stories, both fictitious and real, that portray some aspect of healthcare, and you can safely conclude that North Americans develop their knowledge and attitudes toward healthcare largely from mass media—a conclusion that has been supported time and again by research on media consumption habits.

What this means to healthcare managers is that the media is both a conduit through which your organization may need to get its message to a wide public, and also a gatekeeper that controls what does and does not get a wide audience. The relationship that your organization has with the media can have an effect on both your image and the relationships you have with your community, clients and potential clients, government, donors and potential donors, and even your employees and volunteers.

Some healthcare managers, just like administrative personnel in other industries, believe, mistakenly, that if they simply ignore the media, it will either go away or not affect them. This could not be further from the truth. Regardless of your level within the healthcare hierarchy, there will come a time when either you must face media questions, or at the very least *should* use the media to your best advantage. Thus you can take either a reactive or a proactive stance toward your relationship with the media, but I suggest that you consider developing the attitude that the media needs you just as much as you need its goodwill. Furthermore, it can be a very valuable tool for the development of your organization and even of your own career. If you feel confident about your understanding of the media and in your own personal media relations skills, then you are likely to have a considerably decreased fear of dealing with this often powerful ally (or foe).

WHAT "MEDIA RELATIONS" MEANS IN HEALTHCARE

There is an old saying that you have probably heard before and that every business person worth his or her salt takes very seriously: perception is reality.

What the public (or individuals) believe is true is true for them in all its consequences. Whether or not this perception reflects in any way the actual truth of the situation, the reaction from the public will be based on their "truth" and not yours. How the public comes to develop their perceptions is often a result of media-generated images. In healthcare, this is even more likely to be true. A successful healthcare executive has learned that the one who can communicate messages best to large groups of people is more likely to have those messages received as they were intended.

Whether you like it or not, the public is learning about healthcare from newspapers, magazines, radio, television, and, increasingly, from the Internet. They are receiving images from hard news stories, human-interest dramas, advertising, and television programs like *ER* and *Chicago Hope* (and even afternoon soaps like *General Hospital*). Whether or not you as a healthcare manager consider these appropriate sources of information upon which to base opinions doesn't matter—it is the truth. If you and your healthcare organization have cultivated a beneficial relationship with the media, you may find that you have a degree of influence over how the messages are conveyed and interpreted, at least in your immediate geographic area.

Media relations, then, implies the development of long-term relationships between your organization and the media for mutual benefit. This mutuality means that media cooperation can be very important for you, but your cooperation can also be very useful for the media. The two main benefits of good media relations are: (1) being able to use the media to get a needed message to the public; and (2) increasing the likelihood of balanced coverage in times of crisis or difficulty.

For example: you are the manager of an emergency department or the administrator of a hospital whose overworked emergency department had to send an incoming ambulance patient to another hospital and the patient dies. The media will begin covering the story from the perspective of the "poor little guy"—in this case the patient and his or her family—versus the "big bad guy"—you as a representative of the hospital. A hospital that has cultivated good relationships with the media, and a healthcare manager who is known and trusted by the local media, will have a better chance of a fairer, faster hearing before the story mushrooms out of proportion. But before you can handle an impending crisis like this scenario well, your organization needs to have a well-developed media relations policy.

MEDIA POLICIES IN HEALTHCARE

So, the reporters get a tip about the patient who died after being turned away at your emergency department and they start calling—or worse, arrive on your doorstep. The first person a reporter looks for is a nurse in the emergency department. She starts talking. Then everyone the reporter encounters on his or her way to the official sources talks as well. By the time the reporter reaches you, the story is already juicy enough to go with—never mind that few of the informers had any first-hand knowledge or even the facts.

Do you let just anyone in your institution talk to the media? Have you even thought about it? Do you let reporters into your long-term care facility to begin filming residents any time they like? Do you try to avoid reporters or give them the official "no comment" response? Do you ever tell a media person something that is really not true to get them off your back?

All of these issues must be considered, and organizational policies developed to address them. Media relations policies for five very important areas should be developed and fully communicated to all internal groups.

OFFICIAL SPOKESPERSON

A healthcare organization needs one official spokesperson to deal with calls from the media and to designate others as spokespersons on specific issues as the need arises. Both the individual's position within the organizational hierarchy as well as that individual's media presentation skills should be considered in the selection of this person. In a large organization, this official spokesperson is usually a member of the public relations staff whose title reflects his or her position as media relations officer. Anyone working in such a position should have his or her media presentation skills already examined prior to being hired. In smaller organizations, the official spokesperson is often the administrator or another director if that person's skills are more fully developed. Just because you are the head honcho doesn't necessarily mean that you are the best person for the job. The problem here is that reporters often don't want to talk to the official spokesperson, but the doctor, nurse, or researcher at the front line of the story. The official spokesperson is then responsible for briefing that other person, who is then designated to speak about a particular subject, and only that subject. As a healthcare manager, however, you should be cultivating and nurturing your own media skills so that you are never in a position where you feel intimidated by the media when you are the spokesperson.

COOPERATION AND HONESTY

The second area of concern in the development of media relations policy is taking the view that your organization and its representatives will always be cooperative and honest with the media. The issue of honesty cannot be stressed enough. Any organization that has ever lied to the media has found itself with a very difficult task of rebuilding any trust that might have existed previously. Being cooperative means returning calls when you say you will and providing as much information as is reasonable and ethical given the situation.

CONFIDENTIALITY

The third area of policy derives directly from the issue of openness and honesty and is of particular concern in healthcare organizations: confidentiality of patient information. While you need to have a clear confidentiality policy that is lucidly and calmly related to reporters and media outlets, this cannot be the rule that you continually hide behind in an effort to avoid giving out information to the media. Your policy needs to be very clear about what can and cannot be divulged as a matter of organizational policy.

INTERNAL COMMUNICATION

The next aspect of policy is ensuring that internal audiences receive any information that is being communicated to external audiences before that external communication takes place. No employee or volunteer should ever find out about internal activities via mass media. As a matter of policy, you need to find a way to put the internal groups first. Obviously, in times of crisis, this communication may have to be simultaneous, but the policies and procedures for considering those closest to home first need to be in place.

INTERNAL POLICY

Finally, you need to have a way to communicate these policies to all internal publics. It isn't enough to have a policy that says any employee contacted by the media about any organizational matter must first contact the official spokesperson if the employees don't know that such a policy exists. One of the best ways to communicate these kinds of policies is to develop a media training workshop that provides background information on the media and how to handle situations as they arise. Not everyone needs actual training on how to give a media interview, but everyone could benefit from a better understanding. (Figure 10.1 provides a basic outline of what should be covered in a media training workshop.)

Healthcare managers constantly deal with policies of all kinds. Why shouldn't a good media policy be one of them? Most often, such an omission can be attributed to a lack of understanding of what the media really does and how it is done.

UNDERSTANDING THE MEDIA

Isn't it helpful to know something about what that person on the other end of the phone does? Enhancing your understanding of a reporter's job and the environment within which he or she works helps you to improve your ability to get the right message out at the right time—and can greatly enhance your comfort level. Let's begin by looking in general terms at the reporter's media environment and then more specifically at who that person is and how that person's work is accomplished.

THE MEDIA ENVIRONMENT

In very general terms, it is important to understand that today's media is largely event-oriented rather than issue-oriented when it

FIGURE 10.1   SAMPLE MEDIA TRAINING WORKSHOP OUTLINE

1. Defining "Good Media Relations"
    *   benefits of good media relationships
    *   components of solid media relations policy
    *   a manager's responsibility
2. Health and Healthcare in Media
3. Understanding Media
    *   profile of the journalist
    *   journalistic interview techniques
    *   types of interviews: print, TV, radio
    *   how each medium differs
    *   what makes news
4. The Interview
    *   why you should do the interview
    *   how to prepare for an interview
    *   verbal presentation
    *   non-verbal presentation
    *   what not to do during an interview
5. Dealing with the Confrontational Journalist
6. On-Camera Role Play
    *   each participant is interviewed and taped
    *   each interview is played to the group for evaluation

comes to health-related content. By definition, issues are broader, deeper, and have more long-term influence over our lives. There are many important health-related issues, from healthcare delivery methods to funding and medical research priorities. The media, however, is far more likely to hone in on a specific event as it relates to the issue, even if that specific event is not representative of the broader concerns. This one piece of information can help you to understand why reporters sometimes ask you questions that you think are relatively unimportant. Our understanding of this aspect of the media has been bolstered by research.

In 1988, a media researcher in Britain analyzed the content of 1,397 health-related articles in seven national newspapers. The results pointed directly to the media's orientation toward events rather than issues. The researcher found that 58 percent of the articles were about an event and gave light details of the surrounding issue. A further 16 percent of the articles focused on the event as well, but provided enough information about the related issue to give readers some background. Only 26 percent had a discussion of the issue as their main focus.[3] The conclusion we might draw from this is that even if the event is reported objectively, the reader, viewer, or listener is likely to receive a skewed image of the real situation. It is especially true in health and healthcare reporting that one event is never representative of the entire surrounding issue.

So, how are these decisions made? Why does one story get printed or aired, while another is buried? Why is one story front-page news and another left out entirely?

Every basic news writing textbook used by student journalists has its own list of news values: what criteria are used to determine the newsworthiness of a particular story. Generally, these values include the following:

- *Timeliness.* "News" is related to "new." If it happened last week, it is not likely to be news unless the remainder of its news values overcome this. Indeed, this search for timeliness explains why reporters are on your doorstep before you even know there is a story and why they always have deadlines to drive them.
- *Currency.* This is related to timeliness, but allows for more leeway in when an event actually happened. If the situation is related to an ongoing, current consumer and/or media interest in a particular topic, it has a high level of newsworthiness.

- *Prominence.* The more prominent the individuals involved, the more likely that something is newsworthy. If your next-door neighbor has quadruple by-pass surgery it is not news—unless he happens to be the mayor (or a congressman, or a movie star, etc.).
- *Proximity.* The closer to home an event occurred, the more newsworthy it is. A small story nationally may be a huge story locally. This is also related to prominence. If the chief executive officer of a small, midwest hospital is accused of sexual harassment, the story likely has little news value for national outlets, but it may be front-page news in the local media.
- *Consequences.* If the situation will have significant consequences, it is more newsworthy. If something small that happens in a long-term care facility is likely to have some public policy outcome, it is now newsworthy.
- *Human drama.* We used to refer to this news value as human interest. More and more, however, there also has to be a dramatic component to the story. Healthcare is rife with human interest stories, as well as human dramas.
- *Controversy.* Many journalism textbooks fail to identify this as a real draw for reporters, but anyone who has ever been on the other side of the microphone knows that controversy is compelling to reporters. Indeed, many of us have had the experience of a reporter seeking out a controversy where no apparent one existed.

Knowing about these news values is important to you in two ways. First, it helps you to understand why some stories that you think are important never make it to the front page. Second, it helps you to understand the direction of the questioning that you will inevitably face when a reporter comes calling. In the end, decisions about what plays in the media on any given day are:

. . . consonant with the interests and image of a particular news organization, reporter, or editor. In this regard, the media play a censorship role, and what is concealed may constitute news.[4]

JOURNALISTS ARE PEOPLE, TOO

Once you understand a bit about the environment that guides the work of the media that you see every day, dealing with the media as a healthcare manager requires you to understand something about that person who is asking all the questions.

The face of journalism has changed considerably. Fifty years ago, you would probably have faced a *man* who had learned his trade by coming up through the ranks. He was probably a bit left-wing in his political leanings, and if we are to believe the kernel of truth in any public stereotype, perhaps he was just a bit ill-kempt.

Journalists today are well educated. Most have studied journalism, among other things, at college or university. The person holding a microphone in your face today is just as likely to be a woman and she may be representative of even more diverse backgrounds than you would have faced years ago. Today's journalist is less left-wing (in fact is likely to have political leanings right about in the center), and he or she probably selected journalism as a career for altruistic reasons. This person truly does (or did) want to save the world by bringing truth and justice to the fore.

It can sometimes be difficult when, as an executive, you are faced with a person who believes that he or she has a sacred mission as a seeker of the truth. You need to ensure that you are not put off by the possibility that this person might just take the moral high ground, and it may be difficult for you to reclaim even footing. But the reality is that while it would seem that the traditional value of objectivity in reporting would make that moral high ground unnecessary, today's journalistic imperative is closer to taking the side of the so-called "little guy" against the "big guy" and seeking the story's balance from that initial stance.

This potentially slanted view is an interesting dichotomy for reporters today as they deal with the conflict between their desire to represent the truth as they see it, and their need to be loyal to their profit-seeking bosses. Keep in mind that media outlets (apart from public broadcasting) are not non-profits.

Finally, however, journalists are people who are just doing their jobs. As media trainer and former journalist Ed Shiller says:

> Aside from the stereotype of the reporter as ill-groomed and ill-clothed, one of the most persistent perceptions of your local reporter is that he or she is either out to get a story, no matter whose toes are trampled, or is an unprincipled sensationalist who wants to nail you to the cross . . . but most reporters are not out to get you. They're out to get a legitimate story.[5]

THE MEDIUM IS THE MESSAGE?

If Marshall McLuhan was right and the medium is the message, then it behooves anyone who plans to have any dealings with mass media to understand how each medium differs and can alter the message you intended.

Consider this situation. Years ago, I headed the communication program for a large multi-organ transplant service. The nature of organ procurement and the fact that organ transplantation was still a media darling at the time meant that I spent many hours giving interviews, appearing on television, and answering the public's questions on radio call-in shows, among other things.

I received a call one morning from an enterprising young reporter from a local affiliate of a national television station. It seemed that the reporter had been contacted by the leader of a grass-roots community group that had been lobbying for the implementation of an organ donor registry. I was very familiar with this group, having met with them several times to determine how we could work together. This collaborative approach was tempered by my own research on organ donor registries, focusing on where they had been tried in the past. There were no success stories. However, it was not our habit to squash a community effort to enhance organ donation without a genuine attempt to work together.

The reporter arrived in my office with her cameraman and before we began my on-camera interview, she told me that she had already interviewed the head of the citizen's group and would be using portions of each interview. We started with a general discussion of the organ donation process, yet again, and the notion of an organ donor registry. I related to her some of the information I had gleaned from my research on the topic. When she asked about our apparent lack of action on the development of the registry as this group of concerned citizens wished, I assured her that we had been meeting regularly, and although these registries had never worked in the past, we were interested in cooperating in any way we could with citizens who supported our work. There was no fight here.

I sat in front of my television at six o'clock that evening to see the results of this interview. My twenty-minute interview resulted in two twenty-second clips that had been craftily edited and juxtaposed with remarks made by the leader of the citizens' group so that the story seemed to be one of conflict between the "big hospital complex" that was being non-cooperative and the "good guy" citizens who just wanted to help. Had the interview been live on the radio, the message would have been quite different. Thus, understanding the differences between the different types of media can help you to craft your skills, and anticipate possible misrepresentation.

THE PRINTED WORD

Print media, the granddaddy of all the mass media we are familiar with today, is still an important part of how a large proportion of your publics will receive information about you and your organization. Increasingly, too, your story that appears in the local newspaper will also make it into cyberspace as more and more newspapers have on-line versions. Therefore, the potential reach of your message is even greater than it used to be.

In general terms, the newspaper is looking for what they call "hard news." They want just the facts because the story has a short life span (here today, gone tomorrow). This is still generally true, although many newspapers are increasingly including longer, more in-depth pieces to feed the information needs of their readers, and to compete with other sources of information such as magazines and television.

Magazines, another important print medium, have a longer story life, their stories involve more research on the part of the writers and researchers, and they can present an analysis. A reporter interviewing you for a news story may ask you about some of the background so that he or she can understand, but much of that background will never make it to print. Magazines as well as feature articles (as opposed to hard news) in newspapers can take a more creative approach as they fill up considerably more space.

An interview for print media can be either via the telephone or in person. While the telephone interview generally takes up less of your time, you are at a disadvantage (as is your interviewer) since you can't see their body language and facial expressions. Either way, you can make your points (we will get to that).

LIGHTS, CAMERA...

Television is almost endlessly varied these days. News broadcasts tend to use short stories, much like a newspaper in that they want just the facts, but they prefer to have a visual context and the story is subject to aggressive editing, as my case suggested. The visual aspect of television news stories can sometimes present a challenge to health facilities whose primary responsibility is to protect the privacy of their clients or patients. While a TV crew may wish to walk around and creatively take footage of anything they like, this is impossible. Therefore, your policies must not only cover this possibility, but must also be conveyed to the appropriate media personnel.

Aside from news stories on television, there is a vast array of other types of pieces and shows in which you might become involved. Feature broadcasts, such as news magazine shows, can use either short or long stories, but they always include both visuals as well as talk. The continual, uninterrupted "talking head" is really past its day as audiences have become more sophisticated and visually demanding. These kinds of broadcasts are carefully scripted and the editing is creative, to say the least. An interviewee generally has no idea how this will come out on the other end.

Some kinds of television interviews that you might be asked to do include:

- *The talk show.* These range from your local noon-hour, in-studio discussion with a broadcaster to the confrontational style of talk show that has become popular in recent years. Generally, however, these interviews involve actually sitting down in a studio with an interviewer. As you are being interviewed in this situation, you need to ensure that you talk to the interviewer, not to the camera.
- *The headshot.* The camera will look directly at you while you talk into it apparently to a host whom the audience cannot see. The interviewer's questions are usually edited out. This could be taped in your office, on the street outside your hospital, in the hallway, or, less likely, in the studio.

- *The news magazine.* This will be a more in-depth interview. The crew might even follow you around for a while. They will want to see you in action. Then they will go away and shoot others and edit them together into a television magazine story.
- *The scrum.* This happens when you are confronted with a number of reporters, usually just as you walk out a door from a meeting of one sort or another. It happens to politicians all the time, but it can also happen to you. If you are negotiating with a union for their new contract, if you have made an on-camera presentation to a government inquiry, or if something controversial is happening inside your institution, you will inevitably run into reporters waiting for a comment.
- *The ambush.* This comes from an individual reporter (although it could be more) who waits somewhere (like around a corner as you are walking to your car) to surprise you, usually shoving a microphone or tape recorder in your face to get a comment from you.
- *The double-ender.* This happens when you are actually being interviewed by a broadcaster whose voice you hear through an earpiece and whom you cannot see. To the viewers, it seems that the interviewer is looking directly at you through the magic of a screen beside him or her and that you are looking directly at the interviewer. In fact, you are looking directly into a camera lens. Shift your eyes away for a split second, and the audience will think you are not to be trusted! The greatest difficulty posed here is the need to focus intently on the interviewer's question. In TV outlets using older equipment, there can even be a delay between the time that the audience hears the question and when you hear it, causing you to look just a bit stunned as you listen intently to what the audience perceives as dead air.

RADIO . . . AFTER ALL THESE YEARS

Media opportunities for radio come in almost as many varieties as do those for television. There are similarities in some of the interviews, like scrums and ambushes, except that the audience can't see you. News broadcasts on the radio are very short. Each story runs thirty to sixty seconds and they have an extremely short lifespan. It is a fast-paced, information-oriented environment.

Documentary-type radio shows come and go in popularity. Just now there seems to be a resurgence in audience interest, frequently on public broadcasters. Radio documentaries vary considerably in length and depth of coverage. They do, however, rely heavily on ambient sound. If they want to do a story about an intensive care unit, for example, they will want to record sounds of ventilators swishing, heart monitors beeping, even the loudspeaker if you still have one. These documentaries are carefully scripted and you could be interviewed not only by a broadcaster but also by a background, off-air researcher.

There are essentially four types of radio interviews:

1. *The studio interview*. This is usually for a radio talk show. It will entail a discussion between you and your interviewer. While it might be aired in its entirety, parts of the interview could be taken out for additions to related news stories.
2. *The sound bite*. This is the brief clip of a memorable few words craftily put together that says it all for the interviewer. It is taken from a larger interview, which could be long or short, on the phone or in the studio, or on the street into a tape recorder.
3. *Phone-in shows*. These are obviously live broadcasts, where you are the invited expert in a particular topic area and listeners are asked to call you with their comments and questions. This is especially fertile ground for health-related

topics. You need to be careful what you say, especially if you are being asked for health-related advice. You also need to know if the station has a broadcast delay: can they bleep out a person's comments before they get onto the air? You can do this in a station with a host, or you can do it in your living room on the telephone for an hour, which will sound just like you are sitting beside the host. (I have done call-in shows while on the East coast, for a live broadcast on the West coast.)

4. *Phone interviews.* These are very common types of radio interviews and they can either be live or taped. Live ones are obviously used in their entirety and you need to be immediately available when the producer calls to get you on the line. Taped phone interviews usually allow you to have a brief chat with the interviewer just before you begin. Sometimes you can even start over if there are any problems at the outset.

So, now that you know something about the backstage aspects of the medium that you will be facing, you are ready to answer that call from a reporter. Or are you? Figure 10.2 is a checklist of what to do when a reporter calls. Run through it and then consider your next step.

FIGURE 2   HELP! A Reporter Is Calling

- Stay calm.
- Write down the callers's full name, position, and affiliation.
- Find out the specific purpose of the call.
- Find out what he or she already knows about the issue at hand.
- Ask about the story's deadline.
- If you don't have all the infomation you need, arrange a call-back.
- Write out your central message and two or three important points.
- Ensure that you have the right to be talking to the media about the topic.

YOU'RE ON!

How *are* your skills in dealing with the media? Even the most seasoned public speaker who can absorb audiences in person, or a personable manager who has terrific rapport with his or her employees, often has difficulty in translating those skills to the specialized area of media presentation. Let's examine general aspects of both your verbal and non-verbal presentation and then look at the specifics of what to do when the media call.

VERBAL

The goal of your verbal presentation is to state your message as clearly as possible so that the audience understands and re-members your message.[6] Here are some guidelines that might help.

- *First, know your subject.* Never agree to a media interview on a subject that you know little about. Ensure that you are, indeed, the person to whom the media should be speaking on this subject. Unless you are the CEO, you will need to determine that you have permission from your organization to represent it in the media.
- *Use plain language and speak in relatively short sentences,* each of which should contain only one point. You may think that this is important only when speaking on television or on radio, but it is equally important when giving an interview to a print journalist. Keep in mind that the writer of the story has far less background in this subject than you do and will need to be brought up to speed. Avoid industry jargon and medical or technical terms. If you need to use one, explain it briefly before going on.
- *Overall, make only one to three points,* which should have been prepared before the interview. Do not try to make

things up as you go along. If you make numerous points, you are essentially leaving it up to the reporter to decide on the priorities and his or her decision may not resemble yours at all. You run the risk of diluting your message.

- *Don't spoil the reporter's "quotable quote" or "sound bite"* by either numbering your points or using the reporter's name (in fact, try to avoid using the reporter's name at all). This is obviously more important in broadcast than in print interviews, but it is easier to be consistent.

- *Never lose control of the tone of your voice.* You may be saying more than you intend and the reporter will interpret your comments on the basis of both what you say and how you say it.

- *Never actually say "no comment."* It is useless to everyone and when reported verbatim implies to the readers, viewers, or listeners that you are trying to hide something. Instead, indicate that you are unable to give an answer at this time because of . . . and give a reason.

- *Never say anything to a reporter "off the record."* There is no such thing. Even though a credible reporter will not actually use your comments, the fact that he or she knows something will slant questions he or she may ask you or others. In fact, one of the most interesting reporters' tactics is to seek corroboration from someone else for a fact that cannot be attributed to the original source because it was "off the record." Thus, your comment can end up in the story anyway, even though it may not be attributed to you.

- *Don't ever guess.* If you don't know the answer, offer to find someone who does. Guessing can lead to misinformation and place you and your organization in a negative position.

- *Be completely honest without compromising your organization's need to protect the privacy* of patients, clients, staff, board members, physicians, or anyone else to whom you owe this obligation. Simply stated, never, ever lie to the media.

NON-VERBAL

While all of these suggestions will improve your verbal presentation in an interview situation, your non-verbal presentation has its own issues. Your goal here is to ensure that how the interviewer and/or the audience sees you is congruent with the message that you are trying to convey, as well as the image that you need to project as a representative of your organization. While non-verbal presentation is critical in television interviews because the audience can see you, don't forget your non-verbal communication even when only the interviewer can see you. Here are some mostly television-related suggestions for your non-verbal presentation.

- *Avoid extremes of dress.* This includes color, pattern, and style. Avoid white as it is too reflective for the camera. Men who are being interviewed late in the day should shave before appearing on camera. That so-called "five-o'clock shadow" can make you look sinister. Women should avoid short skirts and both men and women need to remember to pull the back of their jackets down (even sit on the end of it if you can) to avoid that quarterback look. Wear only conservative jewelry and avoid anything that will clink.
- *Be constantly aware of your body language and facial expressions.* How you physically present yourself can speak more loudly than any words that come out of your mouth. Even gestures or expressions you are not aware of can say volumes about you, so be aware of them at all times.
- *Avoid waving your hands around or moving them much at all.* It is very distracting for the audience. If you tend to "talk with your hands" practice being interviewed and have someone videotape you. You may never have this problem again after you have seen yourself.

Even if you are not a hand-talker, it is a terrific idea to have someone videotape you anyway. You might be surprised by what you didn't know about yourself. Do you ever begin your answers with any of these phrases: "I'm glad you asked me that . . .", "Well, let me see . . ." or any other cliché comments? Are you ever impatient at seemingly dumb questions? Do you ever lose your cool? Do you ever lose eye contact with the interviewer? Are your gestures too noticeable? Do you fiddle? Do you say "uh" a lot? You can learn a lot from the exercise.

DEALING WITH A CONFRONTATIONAL REPORTER

The truth is that most of the time it is actually fun to be interviewed. Sometimes, however, especially when you are dealing with a controversial situation, it isn't enjoyable at all, and, like Mother Theresa, you may feel that "It is harder to face the media than to bathe a leper."

As you develop a good rapport with your local journalists and they come to see you as a cooperative and effective interviewee, you will run less risk of facing a truly confrontational reporter. Some reporters, however, have this style about them even on the best days. In addition, a reporter may have a hidden agenda and attempt to get you to say something or corroborate something that isn't immediately apparent. Dealing with these reporters can be a challenge.

First, remain calm. You are the expert and the reporter needs your comments to be able to develop the story. Even if the reporter tries to put you on the defensive, it does you no good to take the bait. Never lose your cool. You can always turn a negative question into a positive answer. When the focus is on a crisis in your organization, for example, focus your answer on the positive steps being taken to deal with the situation.

If the interview is on the telephone, it is even easier to deal with a confrontational reporter. Be very polite and indicate to the reporter that you are out of time but that you would be happy to continue the interview later. This will give you time to prepare.

Many managers in healthcare organizations seem to think that all reporters are likely to be confrontational. This isn't true at all—but from time to time you will face one who is and you need to be prepared.

DO YOU NEED MEDIA TRAINING?

Most healthcare managers should be specifically trained in media presentation at some point in their careers. Certainly, it is necessary for high-level executives in health-related organizations to have more than a passing understanding of the media and how they appear in the media. But is media training cost-effective?

In most cases, the answer to that question is yes. However, the training you need may be available to you from your own public relations staff. If you are part of an organization that is large enough to have such a staff, they should be able to do this. If you are flush with money, you might even consider hiring a specialist from outside your organization who can do this for you and a group of managers. It just might help you avoid public embarrassment in the future.

If you have less money, you might consider tracking down a faculty member from your local college public relations department or corporate communication program. These people often have a great deal of experience and are far less expensive than media training firms. They might not provide as slick a presentation, but it will be just as effective.

What should you expect from a media trainer? You might hire a media trainer for one-on-one counseling, but for a group situation you should have a presentation about the media and how to present yourself, as well as a role-playing experience (as suggested in Figure 10.2). Each participant in such a workshop should have an opportunity to be interviewed, videotaped, and critiqued. This is the part that can make media training expensive.

KEY POINTS

1. Health and healthcare are newsworthy and healthcare managers cannot afford to ignore the media.

2. All healthcare managers should be trained in media presentation as they climb the organizational hierarchy.

3. Healthcare organizations need well-articulated media relations policies that are communicated clearly both internally and to the media.

4. Most health-related stories in the media are event oriented rather than issue oriented, which does not always lend itself to the audience's full understanding of the context.

5. Journalists today are well educated and more diverse in gender, ethnic background, and political leanings.

6. It is important to understand the different types of interviews for various media.

7. Always prepare carefully for a media interview.

8. If media interviews are or should be a part of your job today or in the future, get thee to a media trainer!

NOTES
1. Burkett, W. 1986. *New Reporting: Science, Medicine and High Technology*. Ames, IA: The Iowa State University Press, p. 100.

2. King, M., J. Najarian, D. Trunkey, and C. Mauroudis. 1989. "Medicine and the Media: Social and Legislative Issues Symposium of the Society of University Surgeons." *Surgery* (105) 4, pp. 549–552.
3. Kristiansen, C. 1988. "The British Press's Coverage of Health: An Antagonistic Force." *Media Information Australia* (47), pp. 56–60.
4. Marcos, L. 1989. "Media Power and Public Mental Health Policy." *American Journal of Psychiatry* (146) 9, p. 1186.
5. Shiller, E. 1994. *The Canadian Guide to Managing the Media*, revised ed. Scarborough, Ontario: Prentice Hall Canada Inc., pp. 78–79.
6. Biomedical Communications Inc. 1998. *Tips for Dealing With the Media*. BCI Tip Sheet Series. Halifax, Nova Scotia: Biomedical Communications Inc.

FOR YOUR BOOKSHELF . . .

Fox, James and Jack Levin. 1993. *How to Work with the Media.* Sage.

Schiller, Ed. 1994. *The Canadian Guide to Managing the Media.* Prentice Hall.

ON THE WEB . . .

Module on "Training for T.V."
http://www.mediatraining.net

Tips on Media Relations
http://www.publicity.com

Media Relations Report
http://www.ragan.com/html/main.cgi?sub=291&mag=18

Practical Tips for Interviews
http://www.karenfriedman.com

LEVEL IV

Crises and Issues

Tracking and managing issues—preparing for, dealing with, and preventing crises—are all in a day's work for managers in any industry today, and healthcare is no exception. Frequently, however, managers fail to recognize the strategic value of full consideration of communication in such situations and how their own communication skills and style could affect the outcomes.

In this final level, we will examine communication in crisis and issue situations and take a look at the future of strategic communication for healthcare managers.

Communication in a Crisis

From fortune to misfortune is a short step; from misfortune to fortune is a long way.

— Yiddish proverb

WHEN A CRISIS hits a health-related organization, the managers are front and center. Quite apart from how you manage the operational aspects of the crisis, communication during these times of stress can make or break the success of the operations and have long-term consequences. Communicating during a crisis is not the same as everyday communication. Although it is important to consider all of the same audiences, what you need to say and how you need to say it are two different things. Will you be ready when it hits the fan?

WHAT *IS* A CRISIS, ANYWAY?

Like much modern jargon, the term *crisis* is often used when a less extreme word will do, when the situation is not really a crisis at all. So what actually constitutes a crisis?

179

As you read crisis management literature, you will come to one striking conclusion: everyone who writes about it seems to have a different interpretation of the word. While some authors equate it with disasters and catastrophes,[1] others are very clear that these terms refer to quite different phenomena.[2] Webster's is, however, very clear in its definition about the important characteristic of a crisis: " . . . a turning point in the progress of an affair or of a series of events; a critical moment."[3] It is this quality of the potential for important consequences that turns a situation into a crisis—and most often that situation is indeed derived from a series of events that are already happening.

Public relations professional Albert Tortorella has consulted with a wide variety of organizations facing crises, including Johnson and Johnson during the Tylenol crisis and Union Carbide when it faced its Bhopal tragedy. He put it this way: "A problem which may be on the agenda for future action becomes a crisis when it is pushed into the present ahead of its schedule. Often the pushing . . . comes from the media."[4] It is this vulnerability of public exposure with its potential consequences that forces that issue into the forefront. So, for the purposes of our discussion about healthcare communication during a crisis, we will define a crisis as follows:

> A crisis is an event of considerable urgency that opens a health-related organization to public scrutiny outside its control and which has potentially serious consequences for the organization's image and its ability to fulfill its mission.

In health-related organizations, the potential crises are many, from those that are specific to the healthcare industry, to those that can befall any organization. Here are some examples of crises that have recently occurred in healthcare organizations:

- strikes
- layoffs
- an on-premises shooting
- discovery of a dead doctor in the OR lounge (suicide)
- arrest of a nurse for allegedly killing babies in the NICU
- a lost patient
- a medication error resulting in the death of a patient
- a lawsuit or potential lawsuit
- a bomb threat
- an activist attack on an animal research facility
- alleged misappropriation of funds by a senior manager
- patient/resident bashing
- serious ethical questions about a new technology

Although clearly some of these situations can happen in any kind of an organization, others are specific to health and medicine. The managers who would be involved in these crises include the front-line managers directly involved, as well as their supervisors and, often indirectly, managers on their same level in other departments. As you have probably already figured out, media attention can add considerably to the gravity of the situation from your point of view. Thus, information and how it is communicated are key issues when dealing with a crisis. How you and your organization come across to the public can have more far-reaching consequences than how your organization handles the situation from an operational perspective. Remember: perception is reality.

MAINTAINING CREDIBILITY

"With credibility all things are possible. Without credibility, little can be accomplished."[5] Crises tend to generate a lot of contradictory information from a wide variety of sources, many of which you have no control over. What you can control, however, is the quality of the information coming from your organization and how it is conveyed. How you are perceived by the public during a crisis is its reality; therefore, it is critical for you to appear credible and honest. While being honest and appearing credible are related, they aren't the same thing.

If you and your organization have paid careful attention to your relationships with your community and the media, and you have a reputation for honesty and fairness, you are ahead of the game during a crisis. A solid reputation is one of the most important assets you can take into the public eye in the middle of a crisis. After that, your organization's and your own personal ability to communicate honestly and fairly with the media and other publics during the critical period of time will either enhance or detract from your credibility.

In general, "credibility depends on the public's perception of [the organization's] power, competence, trustworthiness, goodwill, idealism, and dynamism."[6] These factors will play into the way you and your organization are accepted by those who receive any information from you. This includes, but is not limited to, media.

COMMUNICATING DURING A CRISIS

It is widely believed in communications circles that if you don't "go public" within the first three to six hours after a crisis becomes public, you have very little chance of recovering your credibility or of taking control of a situation. Therefore, being prepared for the worst is important. This means that both you and your organization need to think about crises long before they happen.

Communication during a crisis requires three main elements: a plan, a crisis team, and a spokesperson.[7] Having a crisis plan at your fingertips requires continual scanning of your organization's environment to determine possible issues that could escalate into crises. For example, if your hospital has a research facility that uses animals in their work, you would need to be prepared for any escalation of animal-rights activity. This means that your public relations personnel need to be proactive, forging appropriate community relationships and preparing a plan to use should the need arise. This is a specific issue that can escalate. But what if an estranged spouse walks into your staff lounge and shoots his wife? You could not have been expected to be prepared for this specific event which is not unique to healthcare. That is why communication must be an important element in the development of your generic crisis management plan.

Here is what should happen to your organization's communication when a crisis hits:

- Immediately appoint an official spokesperson
- Assemble all the factual and background material available
- Assemble your crisis communication team
- Prepare your key messages (no more than three)
- Respond to the media quickly and efficiently
- Consider all other affected stakeholders and communicate with them quickly (more about this later)
- Never, ever lie to any of your stakeholders
- Avoid prattling on about the issues at hand
- Avoid becoming defensive
- Be proactive and keep control of the communication as much as possible
- Keep your communication simple and free of health, medical, or hospital jargon
- Avoid saying "no comment" and, as usual when dealing with the media, never say anything "off the record"
- Continually monitor how the crisis is being reported in the media

The bottom line is that if you have established a good reputation, enhanced your organization's and your own communication skills, and prepared for the worst, communicating during a crisis is a matter of maintaining your composure and using the skills that you would use on a regular basis. These skills need to be applied not only to media interactions, but to communication with any of your stakeholders whose responses could have an effect on your future relationship with them.

DEALING WITH YOUR STAKEHOLDERS

If you are in the habit of considering the effect of your actions and words on all those groups whose good will is important to your organization, then considering their needs during a crisis will come naturally. However, if you are concerned only with what the media might say, then you will almost certainly cause a deterioration in your relationship with any number of other important publics.

First, consider your employees. As we have discussed previously, they are your most important ambassadors and should be considered as such during a crisis. Ensure that employees are kept informed. If you are a front-line manager, take it upon yourself to become the liaison who accumulates the factual information to quell the rumors that inevitably develop during a crisis. If you are a higher-level manager, then ensure that your front-line managers have the information they need.

If you have a board of directors, careful consideration must be made to keep them in the communication loop. It is possible that the chairman of your board may consider him or herself to be an unofficial spokesperson for your organization. This is a mistake. Board chairs, or board members for that matter, are not involved in the day-to-day activities of your organization and need to be made aware before the fact that their role during a crisis is minimal. If you do have a staff member such as a physician on your board, you need to be very forthright about that person's role in public communication during a crisis.

You will also need to pay attention to other groups during a crisis, assessing their communication needs and strategically responding to their informational requirements. The most important of these groups include your patients or clients and their families, and the community in which you function. These will always be important groups. Then, depending upon the type of crisis, you may also need to consider government or regulatory agencies, activist groups, unions, or any other specifically involved group. Communication with these groups cannot be left to the media. In other words, these groups should receive their information in a less-filtered way from your organization.

Methods used to communicate with these groups vary with the group and your objectives, but perhaps even more important is that the practicalities of a crisis situation may require you to alter your ideal. For example, while it may be strategically optimum for you to speak directly to your internal groups on a daily basis as a lengthy crisis unfolds, this may not be feasible. Thus, you may need to resort to written communication methods such as e-mail.

BEING THE SPOKESPERSON: ARE YOU READY?

Unless you are in the position of chief administrator or director of communication, it is unlikely that you will be the official spokesperson. However, as a healthcare manager, you may be called upon by that official spokesperson to speak for your organization if the crisis directly affects your managerial unit or you are, in fact, the on-site expert about a specific, related issue. In either event, you need to have a handle on your own skills as a spokesperson.

As a spokesperson, the group you will have the most inter-action with is the media. As you do a self-assessment, then, you should go back to the basic media skills that we discussed in Chapter 10. However, during a crisis, while general techniques may be the same, challenges can be heightened.

During a crisis, perhaps more than during any other kind of situation, it is important to ensure that the media "gets it right." This means that monitoring the media is extremely important. Further, it is important to follow up if, indeed, there are errors in the reporting. How do you do this?

First, check your facts, then go directly to the reporter who made the mistake. This is not the time to be lodging a complaint with the Broadcast Standards Council or Press Council. That approach will only serve to anger the reporter and further erode your increasingly frail relationship with him or her. Once you are certain that your complaint has foundation, contact that reporter and calmly and diplomatically describe the nature of your concern: an unbalanced story, a factual error, a misleading slant. Between the two of you, you may be able to determine a mutually agreeable solution.

If the reporter adamantly refuses to see the error as being something that he or she should address, you will then have to consider alternative approaches. This usually involves a pointed letter to the editor (back to your writing skills); or in a very difficult situation, you may have to consider a paid advertise-ment (print or broadcast) from your organization. This, however, has both advantages and disadvantages. The main advantage in an advertisement is that you have complete control over the message, both verbally and visually, and the size of the story that will appear. The disadvantage is that the public often views such advertising skeptically. Without the perception of third-party endorsement, the message loses a degree of cred-ibility. Obviously, the more credible you and your organiza-tion are in the eyes of your community in general, the more likely that any message from you will be perceived as more honest.

What is interesting about strategic communication during a crisis is that a manager's skills in interpersonal and written communication, and the ability to deal with the media, can have long-term effects on the outcomes.

KEY POINTS

1. Communication during a crisis is an important strategic consideration.

2. Managers in healthcare organizations require high-level communication skills to have a positive effect on the outcome of a crisis.

3. Media involvement is almost inevitable in crisis situations.

4. Maintaining credibility with all stakeholder groups is crucial to an organization successfully weathering a crisis.

5. It is important to "go public" within the first few hours during a crisis to maintain control and credibility.

6. Strategic communication during a crisis requires a plan, a crisis team, and a spokesperson.

7. Don't forget about communication with internal groups when a crisis has made a situation public.

NOTES

1. Newsom, D., J. Vanslyke Turk, and D. Kruckeberg. 1996. *This Is P.R.: The Realities of Public Relations*, 6th ed. Belmont, CA: Wadsworth Publishing Company.
2. Brody, E. W. 1991. *Managing Communication Processes: From Planning to Crisis Response.* New York: Praeger.

3. *New Illustrated Webster's Dictionary.* 1992. New York: PMC Publishing Company, Inc., p. 235.
4. Tortorella, A. 1989. "Crisis Communication: If it Had a Precedent, it Wouldn't be a Crisis." *IABC Communication World*, June, p. 42.
5. Brody, *op. cit.*, pp. 181–182.
6. Newsom, et al., *op cit.*, p. 206.
7. *Ibid.*

FOR YOUR BOOKSHELF . . .

Dougherty, Devon. 1992. *Crisis Communication: What Every Executive Needs to Know.* Walker Publishers.

Henry, Rene A. 2000. *You'd Better Have a Hose if You Want to Put Out the Fire: The Complete Guide to Crisis and Risk Communications.* Gollywobbler Productions.

Pinsdorf, Marion. 1999. *Communicating When Your Company Is Under Siege: Surviving Public Crisis.* Fordham University Press.

ON THE WEB . . .

Crisis Communication Plan Tips
http://www.mgma.com/news/pubs/crisis.html

12

Healthcare Communication
for the Future

When they discover the center of the universe, a lot of
people will be disappointed to discover they are not in it.

— Bernard Bailey

NO ORGANIZATION FUNCTIONS in a vacuum. Neither does
the world revolve around any single organization. No matter
how noble the cause, how admirable the work, how worthy the
protagonists, there will always be detractors, critics, and skeptics.
Health-related organizations, perhaps more than any others, and
particularly some health professionals, often suffer from the
mistaken idea that because of the human service aspect of the
work they do, they somehow have a right to the higher moral
ground. This is a dangerous assumption for healthcare managers.
What is needed more than ever before is careful consideration
of how health-related organizations and their managers appear
to the public.

The need for strategic communication in the management of
healthcare activities has grown out of a need for organizations to
communicate their messages expertly to a variety of constituents

189

whose goodwill is important. This goes far beyond trying to persuade publics to your point of view, as we have discussed throughout this book. The behavior of these constituents both directly and indirectly affects the organization's ability to continue pursuing its noble cause, its admirable work, and its overall service to society. And the need for this approach to strategic communication will only intensify, rather than diminish, in the future.

To examine the future of communication within healthcare management we need to broaden our view. Examining the role of health-related organizations within a social context provides us with an expansive canvas upon which to paint a vision of the future. Change is inevitable; therefore, a serviceable starting point is a look at what is likely to be transformed on this canvas. However, some issues are not likely to change a great deal, and these are just as important. Finally, we will look at how the individual healthcare manager can keep his or her communication strategic.

WHAT WILL CHANGE

THE AGING POPULATION

Probably one of the most important factors affecting how healthcare organizations must reconsider how they communicate is the aging population. No one needs the government statistics about the aging baby boomers to recognize that the population is getting older. This situation is particularly acute for healthcare organizations, as health problems increase with age. The communication strategies and approaches of both organizations and individuals will have to change.

First, the age of your employees is edging ever upward: Workers 55 and older are the fastest growing segment of the workforce, with the median age of the workforce projected to reach 40 by 2010.[1] In a society that is still in the grips of a youth obsession—baby boomers trying fruitlessly to hang on to their youthful bodies and skills — it is easy to figure out that the way organizations communicate with the employees will have to change. The situation in healthcare is especially acute, as the workforce through much of the last century was typically younger than in many other industries. Aging employees want information about different things than do younger employees, and healthcare managers have to provide that information in a way that avoids any sense of discrimination.

Clearly, the most important aging group that healthcare organizations need to communicate with is their current and potential patients and clients. If we take a lesson from the marketers, we learn that the actual words we use to communicate with this important group are key to getting their attention.[2] To begin with, it seems that there is no one acceptable term to describe this group. *Senior citizen* is outdated and offensive to some. *Senior* is just as bad. *Old* is discriminatory. *Elderly* conjures up physical frailty. The term *mature* seems to bridge the gap between insulting and non-descriptive.

Once the labeling is out of the way, you will face other communication considerations. One important consideration for more mature audiences is the challenge of finding the right medium to reach them. Hospitals, health-service organizations, and long-term care facilities need to assess the usefulness of the materials they produce and the way these materials and messages are distributed to aging audiences. Here are some questions that may provide useful information in an evaluation of these materials.

1. Is the content applicable to an aging clientele?
2. Is the visual layout considerate to people with declining vision?
3. Is the material distributed in places that are likely to be frequented by aging clients? Or, perhaps, do you use

direct mail (which is considered to be useful for this group)?

PUBLIC OPINION

Another factor that alters communication from healthcare facilities is changing public opinion. Since your organization's image is a reflection of public opinion, how it changes is key to understanding how the external world thinks about you. Public opinion has always been mercurial, but changing demographics of the North American population are likely to magnify this fluctuation. Keeping communication current with public opinion is going to be a challenge for every manager in the healthcare industry.

Everyday it seems, your audiences have more easily accessible information about health and healthcare. This proliferation of health-related information is a double-edged sword. On one hand, it does indeed serve to empower many consumers with enough information to somewhat balance that lopsided relationship that patients have traditionally had with healthcare providers. It truly makes them a part of the decision-making process about their own health status and healthcare decisions. On the other hand, however, a frighteningly large portion of the population has difficulty sifting through all of this available information. They have no frame of reference for determining what is truly useful to them and what is completely inaccurate.

Never before have we had so much genuinely valuable healthcare information so easily accessible. But, thanks in large part to on-line sources, never before have we had access to so much spurious rubbish, either. Healthcare organizations have an increasingly important role to play as credible sources of information. Indeed, it may even be the case that they have a duty to assist consumers in this search for useful information. This might make the basis for a terrific community relations strategy!

INDIVIDUAL ATTITUDES TOWARD HEALTHCARE

Another consequence of this increase in information is that attitudes toward healthcare decision making are changing. Even fifty years ago most decisions about healthcare were happily left to health professionals, mostly doctors. They knew best and paternalism was rampant. Now, however, public attitudes about who should be making these decisions and how they should be implemented are changing.

The communication implications for healthcare organizations are many. Are your employees knowledgeable about patients' rights? Do they have enough materials available to aid them in assisting patients? Are your employees aware of management's perspective on patient decision making? Do your patients/clients know their rights? Is your community familiar with your philosophy? These are just a few of the questions you have to be able to answer.

FAST-FORWARD TECHNOLOGY

Finally, communication technology changes almost daily and is likely to continue to change. Financial concerns notwithstanding, health-related organizations cannot afford to lag behind in communication technology. As a manager, it is important that you first recognize that access to the latest in communication technology is a strategic advantage. Second, you must be comfortable with the use of these technologies. When voicemail was first introduced into our workplaces, there were those who refused to embrace it or even learn how to use it. Then came electronic mail and few of us realized the extent to which it would revolutionize how we communicate. These two examples are only the beginning. Your own knowledge and comfort will enable you to ensure that others within your organization understand that these communication technologies are not only a nice addition to your organization's abilities, but may be crucial for their continued success.

These changes are already happening and, in fact, may be better identified as trends. The bottom line is that the context of communication is continuing to change and healthcare managers need to recognize these changes and adapt their strategies to them.

WHAT WON'T CHANGE

Even amidst all this change, however, some very crucial issues will remain the same—the most important of which is the requirement for organizations of all kinds to recognize their social responsibility. Despite the fact that health-related organizations, by virtue of their very missions, consider their core work to be fulfilling a social responsibility, we need to examine the issue through a broader lens.

All organizations in society continue to exist only if they fulfill a societal need, only if they are serving a useful public interest.[3] While at their core, health-related organizations seem to serve a vital public need, there must always be the public perception that the organization in question is doing so in a socially responsible way. In general, this implies that the organization fulfills its mission within the letter and spirit of the law at all times, has a code of ethics that guides its decision making, and that its activities reflect respect for human dignity and consideration for its larger community—in short, the organization is a good citizen. These actions are more powerful communication tools than any words that might come from your organization.

From time to time, it might be a useful exercise for health-related organizations to perform a social audit. This is a tool that you design to identify and assess your "social and environmental impacts, communicate internally and externally [your] performance, and make continual improvements in such areas as community and customer relations, employment practices, human rights issues, environmental responsibility, and ethical behavior."[4] This definition implies that communication is at the heart of a social audit. The results may help your organization to formulate directions for not only future communication priorities, but for operational priorities as well. Again, public perception of your organization's activities is at the heart of the matter.

KEEPING YOUR COMMUNICATION STRATEGIC

While the broader context of your communication activities and those of your organization continue to change and develop, there are some things that managers need to do to keep their communication strategic. Here are a few ideas.

1. *Ensure that you treat all audiences as special.* We have talked previously about the issue that one size definitely does not fit all. Careful consideration must be given to determining the informational needs and desires of a variety of constituencies for your organization. Indeed, your own communication practices should always consider this, in everything from composing e-mail messages to making public presentations.
2. *Enhance opportunities for two-way communication both internally and externally.* As attitudes about shared decision making and participation continue to change, it is more important than ever for you to consider how much feedback you invite and what you do with it. This needs to be true two-way communication, not lip service to asking for feedback and then ignoring it. Strive to enhance your communications with employees, clients, medical staff, board members, and the community at every opportunity.

3. *Keep up with new advances in media technology.* This may
   even require you to take a course. Even if you are at the
   highest level in your organization, don't rely on others to
   take up the slack here. As we have discussed all along,
   communication is a requirement of everyone and you, as a
   manager, need to have more than a passing acquaintance
   with the new technologies. Right now:
   - Do you know how to send an attachment with an e-mail?
   - Do you know how to open one whose format you are not
     familiar with (without asking your assistant)?
   - Do you know how to conduct a thorough search of the
     Internet?
   - Are you comfortable using a computer-based slide show?
   - Can you develop one yourself to accompany a public
     presentation?
   These are some very simple media technology questions that
   no healthcare manager should answer 'no' to at this point. It
   is the upcoming ones that you may need to take courses in!
4. *Practice and hone your communication skills.* Your own personal skills—writing, presenting, giving media interviews—
   all need to be assessed and updated continually. Make use
   of your public relations staff if you have one available. Look
   for workshops and seminars. Attend communication sessions
   at health management conferences. Read.
5. *Keep an open mind to enhance creativity in healthcare
   communication encounters.* This is necessary on both a
   personal level and on an organizational level. An old way
   of approaching a communication challenge may be just
   that—old. Always be open to new ideas and strategies.
6. *Respect the power of communication.* It has outcomes that
   are both planned and unplanned and you must be aware of
   these at all times. You should never be caught off-guard by
   any consequence of your communications with anyone, at
   any level, in any situation.

ETHICS AND COMMUNICATION

The power of communication is the very reason that ethical considerations are paramount. *Primum non nocere:* First, do no harm. Anyone who has worked in the healthcare industry even for a short time is familiar with the first commandment of ethics — to do good and to do no harm. And communication can indeed be harmful if not approached with a consideration of its ethical underpinnings.

HONESTY

The primary ethical consideration in healthcare communication, as in all other brands of public communication, is the responsibility to be honest in all undertakings. Religious traditions throughout the world, despite their wide differences, all exhort us to be honest. Indeed, integrity in organizational behavior is crucial to maintaining positive relationships with all of your important constituencies. Honesty is one crucial part of integrity, which implies doing the right thing even when no one is watching.

FAIRNESS

Fairness is also important in healthcare communication. Treating all your audiences as if they are important ensures that your communication efforts reflect your respect for them. Fairness implies that all those constituencies will be considered when planning a communication effort and that you will deal with them honestly in all encounters.

POLITENESS

For the healthcare manager personally, behavioral guidelines can enhance the ethical stance of your communication. It seems fitting that we should end our discussion of how communication for healthcare managers goes beyond persuasion with a note about ordinary politeness. It is truly amazing what good manners, which by their very nature imply respect for others, can do in communication encounters. Can you answer 'yes' to all of the following questions?

- Do you always say "thank you" to those who assist you even when it is part of their job?
- Do you always say please?
- Do you never reprimand a subordinate in front of others?
- Is your temper always well controlled?
- Is your language always appropriate and free of vulgarities?
- Do you completely avoid sexist remarks and/or ethnic slurs?
- Do you always refer to others with the degree of formality you expect for yourself?[5]

You need to be able to honestly answer 'yes' to all of these as a basis for integrity and credibility in your communication efforts. Figure 12.1, with your guidelines for behavior, has the last word.

FIGURE 12.1　Rules of Behavior for Healthcare Managers

- Focus on your own work and not on that of others unless you have specific responsibility for their work.
- Be conscientious and honest at all times. This will become a part of your reputation.
- Be cautious about self-disclosure. Employees and peers do not need to know everything about you.
- Give credit where credit is due. Ensure that those you supervise receive credit for their work rather than taking it for yourself.
- Take responsibility for your own actions. Don't pass the buck.
- Subscribe to a code of ordinary politeness.

Adapted from *Health Care Ethics*. 1992. Middletown, OH: Wall and Emerson Inc., by Arthur H. Parsons and Patricia Parsons. Used with permission.

NOTES

1. Capowski, G. 1994. "Ageism: The New Diversity Issue." *Management Review* 83 (10), p. 10.
2. Flanagan, P. 1994. "Don't Call 'Em Old, Call 'Em Customers." *Management Review* 83 (10), pp. 17–21.
3. Bozeman, B. 1987. *All Organizations Are Public*. San Francisco: Jossey-Bass.
4. Parsons, A. and P. Parsons. 1992. "Social Audits and Accountability." *Health Care Ethics*. Middletown, OH: Wall and Emerson, Inc., p. 146.

FOR YOUR BOOKSHELF . . .

Albom, Mitch. 1997. *Tuesdays with Morrie.* Doubleday.

Parsons, Arthur and Patricia Parsons. 1992. *Health Care Ethics.* Wall and Emerson, Inc.

Parsons, Patricia and Arthur Parsons. 1995. *Hippocrates Now! Is Your Doctor Ethical?* University of Toronto Press.

Renesch, John, Bill Degore, and Angeles Arrien (eds.). 1998. *The New Bottom Line: Bringing Heart and Soul to Business.* New Leaders Press.

ON THE WEB . . .

Corporate Social Responsibility
http://www.bsr.org/bsr

Ageism: What Is It?
http://www.geriatricspt.org/pubs/gerinotes/Sep1996/ageism.html

Physicians for Social Responsibility
htto://www.psr.org

About the Author

PATRICIA PARSONS IS an associate professor and past chairman of the bachelor of public relations degree program at Mount Saint Vincent University in Halifax, Nova Scotia, Canada, where she teaches strateic planning in public relations, media relations, communication ethics, and persuasive writing. Over the past twelve years, she has been a medical writer for both the professional, academic, and lay press in Canada and the United States. She is the author or co-author of six previous books on health and communication issues.

Ms. Parsons is also a medical communications consultant at Biomedical Communications, Incorporated, whose services include public relations planning and implementation, media relations training, development of patient/client education and promotional materials, and personal development services including writing and presentational skills development.

Ms. Parsons received a master's of science degree in Health Education from Dalhousie University, Halifax, Nova Scotia, and is accredited in public relations (APR).